TEACHER'S PET PUBLICATIONS

LITPLAN TEACHER PACK
for
Night
based on the book by
Elie Wiesel

Written by
Barbara M. Linde, MA Ed.

© 1998 Teacher's Pet Publications
All Rights Reserved

ISBN 978-1-60249-218-9

This **LitPlan** for Elie Wiesel's
Night
has been brought to you by Teacher's Pet Publications, Inc.

Copyright Teacher's Pet Publications 1998
11504 Hammock Point
Berlin MD 21811

Only the student materials in this unit plan (such as worksheets, study questions, puzzles, and tests) may be reproduced multiple times for use in the purchaser's classroom.

For any additional copyright questions,
contact Teacher's Pet Publications.

www.tpet.com

TABLE OF CONTENTS *Night*

Introduction	6
Unit Objectives	8
Unit Outline	9
Reading Assignment Sheet	10
Study Questions	11
Quiz/Study Questions (Multiple Choice)	21
Pre-Reading Vocabulary Worksheets	33
Lesson One (Introductory Lesson)	47
Writing Assignment 1	49
Writing Evaluation Form	50
Nonfiction Assignment Sheet	51
Writing Assignment 2	59
Oral Reading Evaluation Form	62
Extra Writing Assignments/Discussion ??	70
Quotations	73
Writing Assignment 3	76
Vocabulary Review Activities	77
Unit Review Activities	78
Unit Tests	85
Unit Resource Material	119
Vocabulary Resource Material	141

A FEW NOTES ABOUT THE AUTHOR
Elie Wiesel

WIESEL, Eliezer 1928-

Elie Wiesel was born on September 20, 1928, in Sighet, Transylvania. His parents owned and operated a store, and his mother was also a teacher. He credits his maternal grandfather with his love of storytelling. As a child and adolescent, Wiesel studied the Talmud, Hasidism, and the Kabala. During the years when he was studying so seriously, he thought it was a waste of time to read novels.

Just after Passover in 1944, when Wieisel was 15, the Nazis sent all of the Jews in Singhet to the concentration camp at Auschwitz-Birkenau. He and his father were later transferred to Buchenwald. He was 16 when the war ended and he was released. Wiesel traveled to France and was reunited with his two older sisters.

Wiesel studied at the Sorbonne from 1948 until 1951. He learned the French language and took courses in literature, psychology, and philosophy. He tutored other students, directed a church choir, and worked as a translator to support himself.

Soon after his release from the concentration camps, Wiesel realized that he had a duty as a survivor to let others know what had happened. He was encouraged in this endeavor by Francios Muriac, a Catholic writer whom Wiesel met in Israel. Wiesel's first book, *And the World Has Remained Silent*, was published in Yiddish in 1956. The abridged, autobiographical version, *Night*, was published in Paris in 1958. Since then it has been translated into eighteen languages and is his best-known work.

Wiesel traveled to the United States in 1956 to write about the United Nations. He was hit by a taxi cab in Times Square. Since he was unable to return to France to renew his residency papers, he instead applied for United States citizenship. He married another Holocaust survivor, Marion Erster Rose, in New York in 1969.

In 1976 Wiesel became the Andrew W. Mellen Professor in Humanities at Boston University. President Carter named him the chairman of the President's Commission on the Holocaust and the chairman of the U.S. Holocaust Memorial Council.

Wiesel has received numerous awards and honors. In 1986 alone he was awarded the Nobel Peace Prize, the Freedom Cup Award from the Women's League for Israel, the Jacob Javits Humanitarian Award of the UJA Young Leadership, and the Medal of Liberty. He holds membership in many societies including the Authors League, a lifetime membership in the Foreign Press Association, American Gathering of Jewish Holocaust Survivors, and the Writers and Artists for Peace in the Middle East. He continues to write and speak for peace and the humanitarian treatment of all peoples.

SELECTED WRITINGS BY ELIE WIESEL

Note: Elie Wiesel writes in French. His works are translated into English by his wife. Only the English titles are given in this list.

Year	Title
1956	*And the World Has Remained Silent*
1958	*Night*
1960	*Dawn*
1962	*The Town Beyond the Wall*
1964	*The Gates of the Forest*
1966	*Legends of Our Time*
1966	*The Jews of Silence: A Personal Report on Soviet Jewry*
1970	*Beggar in Jerusalem*
1970	*One Generation After*
1972	*Souls on Fire: Portraits and Legends of Hasidic Masters*
1973	*The Oath*
1976	*Messengers of God: Biblical Portraits and Legends*
1978	*A Jew Today*
1978	*Dimension of the Holocaust (with others)*
1980	*Images from the Bible*
1981	*The Testament*
1982	*Somewhere a Master: Further Hasidic Portraits and Legends*
1983	*The Golem: The Story of a Legend as Told by Elie Wiesel*
1985	*The Fifth Son*
1985	*Against Silence: The Voice and Vision of Elie Wiesel*
1988	*Twilight*
1988	*The Six Days of Destruction (with Albert Frielandaer)*

INTRODUCTION *Night*

This unit has been designed to develop students' reading, writing, thinking, listening and speaking skills through exercises and activities related to *Night* by Elie Wiesel. It includes seventeen lessons, supported by extra resource materials.

The **introductory lesson** introduces students to background information about places, people, and events mentioned throughout this novel. Since being familiar with the world events at the time of the novel is essential for full understanding, the students will begin the unit with a short research project. This project is used as the first writing assignment and the nonfiction assignment.

The **reading assignments** are approximately twenty pages each; some are a little shorter while others are a little longer. Students have approximately 15 minutes of pre-reading work to do prior to each reading assignment. This pre-reading work involves reviewing the study questions for the assignment and doing some vocabulary work for 8 to 10 vocabulary words they will encounter in their reading.

The **study guide questions** are fact-based questions; students can find the answers to these questions right in the text. These questions come in two formats: short answer or multiple choice. The best use of these materials is probably to use the short answer version of the questions as study guides for students (since answers will be more complete), and to use the multiple choice version for occasional quizzes. It might be a good idea to make transparencies of your answer keys for the overhead projector.

The **vocabulary work** is intended to enrich students' vocabularies as well as to aid in the students' understanding of the book. Prior to each reading assignment, students will complete a two-part worksheet for approximately 8 to 10 vocabulary words in the upcoming reading assignment. Part I focuses on students' use of general knowledge and contextual clues by giving the sentence in which the word appears in the text. Students are then to write down what they think the words mean based on the words' usage. Part II gives students dictionary definitions of the words and has them match the words to the correct definitions based on the words' contextual usage. Students should then have an understanding of the words when they meet them in the text.

After each reading assignment, students will go back and formulate answers for the study guide questions. Discussion of these questions serves as a **review** of the most important events and ideas presented in the reading assignments.

After students complete extra discussion questions, there is a **vocabulary review** lesson which pulls together all of the separate vocabulary lists for the reading assignments and gives students a review of all of the words they have studied.

Following the reading of the book, a lesson is devoted to the **extra discussion questions/writing assignments**. These questions focus on interpretation, critical analysis and personal response, employing a variety of thinking skills and adding to the students' understanding of the book. These questions are done either **independently** or as a **group activity**. Using the information they have acquired so far through individual work and class discussions, students get together to further examine the text and to brainstorm ideas relating to the themes of the novel.

The group activity is followed by a **reports and discussion** session in which the groups share their ideas about the book with the entire class; thus, the entire class gets exposed to many different ideas regarding the themes and events of the book.

There are three **writing assignments** in this unit, each with the purpose of informing, persuading, or having students express personal opinions. The first assignment is to **inform**: students will write a research report on some aspect of the Holocaust or World War II. The second assignment is to express a personal **opinion**: students will keep a response journal while they read. The third assignment is to persuade: students will either persuade the Wiesel family to take refuge with their former servant, or persuade Mr. Wiesel and Elie to stay in the hospital when the camp is evacuated.

Students will use one of their research sources for Writing Assignment #1 to fulfill the requirements for the **nonfiction reading assignment.** Students will fill out a worksheet on which they answer questions regarding facts, interpretation, criticism, and personal opinions. During one class period, students make **oral presentations** about the nonfiction pieces they have read. This not only exposes all students to a wealth of information, it also gives students the opportunity to practice **public speaking**.

The **review lesson** pulls together all of the aspects of the unit. The teacher is given four or five choices of activities or games to use which all serve the same basic function of reviewing all of the information presented in the unit.

The **unit tes**t comes in two formats: all multiple choice-matching-true/false or with a mixture of matching, short answer, and composition. As a convenience, two different tests for each format have been included.

There are additional **support materials** included with this unit. The **unit and vocabulary resource materials sections** include suggestions for an in-class library, crossword and word search puzzles related to the novel, and extra vocabulary worksheets. There is a list of **bulletin board ideas** which gives the teacher suggestions for bulletin boards to go along with this unit. In addition, there is a list of **extra class activities** the teacher could choose from to enhance the unit or as a substitution for an exercise the teacher might feel is inappropriate for his/her class. **Answer keys** are located directly after the **reproducible student materials** throughout the unit. The student materials may be reproduced for use in the teacher's classroom without infringement of copyrights. No other portion of this unit may be reproduced without the written consent of Teacher's

UNIT OBJECTIVES *Night*

1. Through reading *Night* students will analyze characters and their situations to better understand the themes of the novel.

2. Students will demonstrate their understanding of the text on four levels: factual, interpretive, critical, and personal.

3. Students will practice reading aloud and silently to improve their skills in each area.

4. Students will enrich their vocabularies and improve their understanding of the novel through the vocabulary lessons prepared for use in conjunction with it.

5. Students will answer questions to demonstrate their knowledge and understanding of the main events and characters in *Night*.

6. Students will study mood, conflict, sequence, and figurative language through a series of minilessons throughout the unit.

7. Students will completed a nonfiction reading assignment related to *Night*.

8. Students will practice writing through a variety of writing assignments.

9. The writing assignments in this unit have several purposes:
    a. To check the students' reading comprehension
    b. To make students think about the ideas presented by the novel
    c. To make students put those ideas into perspective
    d. To encourage critical and logical thinking
    e. To provide the opportunity to practice good grammar and improve students' use of the English language.

10. Students will read aloud, report, and participate in large and small group discussions to improve their public speaking and personal interaction skills.

UNIT OULINE *Night*

1 Unit Introduction Writing Assignment #1 Nonfiction Assignment	2 Library/ Research Papers	3 Writing Conferences Research Papers	4 Nonfiction Presentations	5 Distribute Unit Materials PVR Section 1
6 ?s Section 1 Writing Assignment #2 Minilesson: Mood	7 PVR Sections 2-3 Oral Reading Evaluation	8 ?s Sections 2-3 PVR Section 4 Minilesson: Conflict	9 ?s Section 4 Minilesson: Figurative Language PVR Section 5	10 Read Section 5 ?s Section 5
11 PVR Sections 6-9	12 ?s Sections 6-9 Minilesson: Sequence	13 Extra Discussion Questions Quotations	14 Writing Assignment #3 Persuade	15 Vocabulary Review
16 Unit Review	17 Unit Test			

Key: P=Preview Study Questions   V=Do Vocabulary Work   R=Read

READING ASSIGNMENTS *Night*

Note to the Teacher: This unit plan was developed using the Bantam Books paperback edition of *Night*. There are no numbered chapter or section divisions in this edition. We have assigned section numbers based on the printed section breaks.

Date to be Assigned	Chapters	Completion Date
		(Prior to class on this date)
	Section 1, pages 1-20	
	Sections 2, 3, pages 21-43	
	Section 4, pages 45-62	
	Section 5, pages 63-80	
	Sections 6, 7, 8, 9, pages 81-109	

WRITING ASSIGNMENTS

Date to be Assigned	Writing Assignment	Completion Date
		(Prior to class on this date)
	Writing to Inform	
	Writing to Persuade	
	Writing to Express a Personal Opinion	
	Nonfiction Assignment	

STUDY GUIDE QUESTIONS

STUDY QUESTIONS *Night*

Section 1, Pages 1-20

1. Describe Moshe the Beadle.
2. Describe Elie Wiesel's father. What was his occupation?
3. Why was Moshe the Beadle important to Elie Wiesel?
4. Summarize the story Moshe the Beadle told on his return from being deported. Why did he say he had returned to Sighet?
5. What was the public reaction to Moshe's story?
6. What was the setting and the year for the first section of the book? What was the world condition at the time?
7. Describe, in order, the events that happened from the last day of Passover until Pentecost.
8. How did Wiesel say he felt about the Hungarian police?
9. Who was Martha? What happened when she visited the Wiesel family in the ghetto?

Sections 2, 3, Pages 21-43

1. To what did Wiesel compare the world?
2. What did Madame Schächter see in her vision?
3. How did the other people in the car react to Madame Schächter?
4. Where did the train stop?
5. What did the Jews in the train car discover when they looked out the window?
6. When did Wiesel say the travelers left their illusions behind?
7. Which notorious SS officer did they meet at Auschwitz?
8. What was Elie's main thought as the men and women were being herded from the train?
9. What prayer were the people saying? Why was it unusual?
10. What did Elie do when the gypsy struck his father? Why? What was his father's response?
11. How long were Elie and his father at Auschwitz? Where did they go after that?

Section 4, Pages 45-62

1. Describe Elie's encounter with the dentist.
2. What did Elie Wiesel do when Idek hit his father? What was he thinking?
3. Who took Elie's gold tooth? Why did Elie give it up?
4. What were the only things in which Elie took an interest?
5. How did Elie describe the men after the air raid?
6. What happened to the young man from Warsaw? Why?
7. How did Elie say the soup tasted the night the *pipel* (young servant boy) was hanged?

Section 5, Pages 63-80

1. What did the men do on the eve of Rosh Hashana?
2. How did Elie feel while the others were praying?
3. What was Elie's decision about fasting on Yom Kippur? Why did he make that decision?
4. What was Elie's "inheritance" from his father? Why was his father giving it to him?
5. Did the men remember to say the Kaddish for Akiba Drumer?
6. What did Elie dream of when he dreamed of a better world?
7. What happened to the patients who stayed in the hospital instead of being evacuated?
8. What was the last thing the head of the block ordered the men to do before they evacuated? Why?
9. What was the weather like during the evacuation?

Sections 6, 7, 8, 9, Pages 81-109

1. While running, an idea began to fascinate Elie. What was the idea? What kept him from carrying out his idea?
2. What did Elie realize about Rabbi Eliahou and his son?
3. What was the name of the camp to which the men walked?
4. Describe Elie's meeting with Juliek.
5. How long were they at Gleiwitz? Where did they go next?
6. Who was Meir Katz? What happened to him?
7. How many men started out in the train? How many were left when they arrived at Buchenwald?
8. What happened to Mr. Wiesel, Elie's father?
9. What was Elie's only desire?
10. What happened on April 10, 1945?

KEY: SHORT ANSWER STUDY QUESTIONS *Night*

Section 1, Pages 1-20

1. Describe Moshe the Beadle.
    He worked at the Hasidic synagogue. He was able to make himself seem insignificant, almost invisible. He was timid, with dreamy eyes, and did not speak much.

2. Describe Elie Wiesel's father. What was his occupation?
    He was cultured and unsentimental. He had more concern for outsiders than for his own family. He and his wife were storekeepers.

3. Why was Moshe the Beadle important to Elie Wiesel?
    Moshe became his cabbalist, or instructor in the mystical aspects of the Jewish faith.

4. Summarize the story Moshe the Beadle told on his return from being deported. Why did he say he had returned to Sighet?
    He and the other foreign Jews had been taken by train through Hungary and into Poland. They were taken to a forest and made to dig graves. Then the Gestapo killed them. Moshe escaped because he had been mistaken for dead, although he was just wounded. He said he returned to tell the Jews to prepare themselves before it was too late.

5. What was the public reaction to Moshe's story?
    People refused to believe him. Some would not even listen to him. They said he just wanted their pity.

6. What was the setting and the year for the first section of the book? What was the world condition at the time?
    The year was 1942. The story started out in the town of Sighet in Transylvania. World War II was in progress. The author mentions 1943, then describes events in 1944. The Fascist party had taken power.

7. Describe, in order, the events that happened from the last day of Passover until Pentecost. On the seventh day of Passover the Germans arrested the Jewish community leaders. The Jewish residents were not allowed to leave their houses for three days. At the end of the three days the Jews had to start wearing the yellow star. Then two ghettos were set up. On the Saturday before Pentecost, Stern attended an extraordinary meeting of the council. When he returned he told the others they were all to be deported, starting the next day.

8. How did Wiesel say he felt about the Hungarian police?
> He said he began to hate them because they were his and his community's first oppressors.

9. Who was Martha? What happened when she visited the Wiesel family in the ghetto?
> Martha was a former servant of the Wiesel family. She visited the family in the ghetto and offered them safe refuge in her village. Elie's father refused to leave. He told Elie and his sisters they could go, but they refused to be separated.

Sections 2, 3, Pages 21-43

1. To what did Wiesel compare the world?
> He said it was a cattle wagon hermetically sealed.

2. What did Madame Schächter see in her vision?
> She said she saw a fire--a furnace, with huge flames.

3. How did the other people in the car react to Madame Schächter?
> Some of the young men tied her up and gagged her. Then they hit her. The others encouraged the young men.

4. Where did the train stop?
> It stopped at Auschwitz. Alternate answer: It arrived at Birkenau, the reception center for Auschwitz.

5. What did the Jews in the train car discover when they looked out the window?
> They saw flames gushing out of a tall chimney into the sky.

6. When did Wiesel say the travelers left their illusions behind?
> It was when they left the train at Birkenau. They left their cherished objects and illusions behind on the train.

7. Which notorious SS officer did they meet at Auschwitz?
> They met Dr. Mengele.

8. What was Elie's main thought as the men and women were being herded from the train?
> It was to stay with his father at all costs.

9. What prayer were the people saying? Why was it unusual?
> They were reciting the Kaddish. It was unusual because they were saying the prayer for the dead for themselves.

10. What did Elie do when the gypsy struck his father? Why? What was his father's response? He did not do anything. He felt remorse, and thought he would never forgive the gypsy. His father whispered that the blow did not hurt.

11. How long were Elie and his father at Auschwitz? Where did they go after that?
> They were at Auschwitz for about three weeks. Then they went to Buna.

Section 4, Pages 45-62

1. Describe Elie's encounter with the dentist.
> The dentist wanted to take out Elie's gold tooth. Twice Elie said he was ill, and the dentist did not take the tooth. Then the dentist was arrested and his office was closed.

2. What did Elie Wiesel do when Idek hit his father? What was he thinking?
> Elie did not do anything to help his father. He was trying to keep from getting hit himself. He was angry at his father for not avoiding Idek's punishment.

3. Who took Elie's gold tooth? Why did Elie give it up?
> Franek, the foreman, wanted the tooth. When Elie refused, Franek began tormenting Elie's father. After two weeks, Elie gave him the tooth.

4. What were the only things in which Elie took an interest?
> He only took an interest in his soup and his crust of stale bread.

5. How did Elie describe the men after the air raid?
> He said they inhaled the smokey air and their eyes shone with hope.

6. What happened to the young man from Warsaw? Why?
> He was hanged for stealing during the air-raid.

7. How did Elie say the soup tasted the night the *pipel* (young servant boy) was hanged?
> He said it tasted of corpses.

Section 5, Pages 63-80

1. What did the men do on the eve of Rosh Hashana?
    They held their prayer service and later wished each other a Happy New Year.

2. How did Elie feel while the others were praying?
    He felt strong, and said he had stopped pleading. He was not able to feel sorrow. He observed the prayer service like a stranger.

3. What was Elie's decision about fasting on Yom Kippur? Why did he make that decision? He did not fast. One reason was because his father had forbidden him to fast. The other reason was that he saw his gesture as an act of rebellion against God.

4. What was Elie's "inheritance" from his father? Why was his father giving it to him?
    The inheritance was a knife and spoon. Mr. Wiesel had been selected. He was giving his only possessions to his son before his death.

5. Did the men remember to say the Kaddish for Akiba Drumer?
    No, they did not.

6. What did Elie dream of when he dreamed of a better world?
    He imagined a world with no bells.

7. What happened to the patients who stayed in the hospital instead of being evacuated?
    They were liberated by the Russians two days after the others left.

8. What was the last thing the head of the block ordered the men to do before they evacuated? Why?
    He ordered them to clean the block. He said he wanted the liberating army to know the men who had lived there were not pigs.

9. What was the weather like during the evacuation?
    It snowed the entire time.

Sections 6, 7, 8, 9, Pages 81-109

1. While running, an idea began to fascinate Elie. What was the idea? What kept him from carrying out his idea?
    The idea of death began to fascinate him. The only thing that kept him from trying to die was his father's presence.

2. What did Elie realize about Rabbi Eliahou and his son?
    He realized that the son had been trying to lose his father as the men were all running during the evacuation. At the same time, the Rabbi was looking for his son.

3. What was the name of the camp to which the men walked?
    It was Gleiwitz.

4. Describe Elie's meeting with Juliek.
    The prisoners had arrived at Gleiwitz, and were moving into the barracks. Men were pushing and trampling over each other. Elie heard a voice that he recognized. It was Juliek, the musician from Warsaw who had played the violin at Buna. They spoke for a few seconds. Juliek then played a Beethoven concerto on his violin. The next morning Juliek was dead and the violin had been trampled.

5. How long were they at Gleiwitz? Where did they go next?
    They were at Gleiwitz for three days. Then they traveled by train for ten days until they reached Buchenwald.

6. Who was Meir Katz? What happened to him?
    He was a friend of Mr. Wiesel's. He had been the gardener at Buna. His son had been taken during the first selection, but he had remained sane. Now he was cracking up. He died in the train just before the men were unloaded at Buchenwald.

7. How many men started out in the train? How many were left when they arrived at Buchenwald?
    One hundred men started out. About twelve were left.

8. What happened to Mr. Wiesel, Elie's father?
    He had dysentery and was very ill for a week. Then he died (at Buchenwald) on January 29, 1945.

9. What was Elie's only desire?
>	He wanted to eat.

10. What happened on April 10, 1945?
>	The resistance fighters took charge of the camp. At 6 PM the first American troops arrived.

MULTIPLE CHOICE STUDY/QUIZ QUESTIONS *Night*

Section 1, Pages 1-20

1. Which sentence does **not** describe Moshe the Beadle?
    A. He worked at the Hasidic synagogue.
    B. He was able to make himself seem insignificant, almost invisible.
    C. He was Aryan, not Jewish.
    D. He was timid, with dreamy eyes, and did not speak much.

2. Which sentence does **not** describe Elie Wiesel's father?
    A. He was the most learned man in the town.
    B. He was cultured and unsentimental.
    C. He had more concern for outsiders than for his own family.
    D. He was a storekeeper.

3. Why was Moshe the Beadle important to Elie Wiesel?
    A. Moshe taught Elie to read.
    B. Moshe was the only person who understood Elie's feelings.
    C. Moshe inspired Elie to make plans to leave Singhet and study at a university.
    D. Moshe became his cabbalist, or instructor in the mystical aspects of the Jewish faith.

4. What did Moshe the Beadle tell the people on his return from being deported?
    A. The foreign Jews were made to dig coal to fill the large furnaces.
    B. The foreign Jews were shot and dumped into large mass graves.
    C. The foreign Jews were sent on a boat to Palestine.
    D. The foreign Jews who had money were able to buy their freedom.

5. True or False: Many of the people believed Moshe's story and prepared to leave Singhet.
    A. True
    B. False

6. What was the setting and the year for the first section of the book?
    A. 1935-1939 in Prague, Czechoslovakia
    B. 1950-1952 in Palestine and Jerusalem
    C. 1910-1915 in Berlin, Germany
    D. 1942-1944 in Sighet, Transylvania

7. List, in order, the events that happened from the last day of Passover until Pentecost.
    A. Two ghettos were set up.
    B. The Jews had to start wearing the yellow star.
    C. The Germans arrested the Jewish community leaders.
    D. The Jewish residents were not allowed to leave their houses for three days.

8. Elie Wiesel said he began to hate them because they were his and his community's first oppressors. Who were they?
    A. the Gestapo officers
    B. the Hungarian police
    C. the members of the Jewish council
    D. their non-Jewish neighbors

9. True or False: Elie's mother and sisters went to Martha's village.
    A. True
    B. False

Sections 2, 3, Pages 21-43

1. To what did Wiesel compare the world?
    A. He compared it to a blind and deaf person.
    B. He compared it to a large hole in the ground.
    C. He compared it to a cattle wagon hermetically sealed.
    D. He compared it to the Bible story of the Jews in slavery in Egypt.

2. What did Madame Schächter see in her vision?
    A. She saw large open graves full of children.
    B. She saw a fire--a furnace, with huge flames.
    C. She saw row after row of empty houses.
    D. She saw the face of Hitler laughing at the entire world.

3. True or False: Some of the young men tied Madame Schächter up and gagged her. Then they hit her.
    A. True
    B. False

4. What did the Jews in the train car discover when they looked out the window?
    A. They saw several large factories surrounded by barbed wire fences.
    B. They saw lines of soldiers with truncheons, ready to beat them as they got off.
    C. They saw flames gushing out of a tall chimney into the sky.
    D. They saw wagons full of dead bodies.

5. What did Wiesel say about the travelers' illusions?
    A. They left their illusions in the ghetto in Sighet.
    B. They were still clinging to their illusions even though they gave up their possessions.
    C. They left their cherished objects and illusions behind on the train.
    D. Seeing the German soldiers made them give up their illusions.

6. Which notorious SS officer did they meet at the concentration camp?
    A. They met Hitler himself.
    B. They met Eichman.
    C. They met General Kolomaye.
    D. They met Dr. Mengele.

7. What was Elie's main thought as the men and women were being herded from the train?
    A. It was to stay with his father at all costs.
    B. It was to keep his faith in God.
    C. It was to stay alive and healthy.
    D. It was to be as brave as possible.

8. True or False: The people were reciting the Kaddish, the prayer for the dead, for themselves.
    A. True
    B. False

9. True or False: Elie beat up the gypsy who struck his father.
    A. True
    B. False

10. Which statement is true?
    A. They went to Birkenau, then to Bergen-Belsen, then to Auschwitz.
    B. They stayed at Nuremberg for one month.
    C. They stayed at Galicia for six days, then went to Birkenau.
    D. They were at Auschwitz for about three weeks. Then they went to Buna.

Section 4, Pages 45-62

1. True or False: The dentist gave Elie a gold crown for one of his rotten teeth.
    A. True
    B. False

2. What did Elie Wiesel do when Idek hit his father?
    A. Elie did not do anything to help his father.
    B. He hit Idek over the head with a chair.
    C. He prayed out loud for forgiveness for Idek.
    D. He hit his father himself for not avoiding Idek's punishment.

3. What did Franek want from Elie?
    A. He wanted Elie's new shoes.
    B. He wanted the money Elie was hiding in the hem of his pants.
    C. He wanted Elie's gold tooth.
    D. He wanted Elie's blanket.

4. True or False: Elie gave up the item to keep Franek from tormenting his father.
    A. True
    B. False

5. What were the only things in which Elie took an interest?
    A. He only took an interest in sleep and prayer.
    B. He only took an interest in his and his father's health.
    C. He only took an interest in counting the days until he could get out.
    D. He only took an interest in his soup and his crust of stale bread.

6. True or False: Elie said the men were more depressed than ever after the air raid.
    A. True
    B. False

7. What happened to the young man from Warsaw?
    A. He was tortured and hanged for hitting an SS officer.
    B. He was electrocuted when he tried to climb over the fence.
    C. He was hanged for stealing during the air-raid.
    D. He was shot while trying to escape.

8. How did Elie say the soup tasted the night the *pipel* (young servant boy) was hanged?
    A. He said it tasted delicious.
    B. He said he did not even taste it.
    C. He said it tasted of corpses.
    D. He said it tasted like blood.

Section 5, Pages 63-80

1. When did the men hold their prayer service and wish each other a Happy New Year?
    A. on the eve of Rosh Hashana
    B. on the first day of Hanukkah
    C. on Yom Kippur
    D. on December 31

2. True or False: Elie said he observed the prayer service like a stranger.
    A. True
    B. False

3. What was Elie's decision about fasting on Yom Kippur? Why did he make that decision?
    A. He fasted because it was the right thing to do.
    B. He did not fast, partly as an act of rebellion against God.

4. What was Elie's inheritance from his father?
    A. The inheritance was a few diamonds Mr. Wiesel had hidden in the heel of his shoe.
    B. The inheritance was a gold watch and chain.
    C. The inheritance was a knife and spoon.
    D. The inheritance was a long underwear and a pair of socks.

5. Why was his father giving it to him?
    A. Mr. Wiesel had been selected. He was giving it to his son before his death.
    B. Mr. Wiesel thought Elie might be able to buy his freedom.
    C. Mr. Wiesel wanted Elie to be comfortable.
    D. Mr. Wiesel thought Elie had a better chance of hiding the things than he did.

6. Did the men remember to say the Kaddish for Akiba Drumer?
    A. Yes, they did.
    B. No, they did not.

7. What did Elie dream of when he dreamed of a better world?
    A. He imagined a world without German soldiers.
    B. He imagined a soup pot that was always full.
    C. He imagined all people living in peace.
    D. He imagined a world with no bells.

8. What happened to the patients who stayed in the hospital instead of being evacuated?
   A. The local townspeople took care of them until the end of the war.
   B. They all died of starvation.
   C. They were liberated by the Russians two days after the others left.
   D. They were murdered by the Germans before they left.

9. What was the last thing the head of the block ordered the men to do before they evacuated?
   A. He ordered them to burn all of the buildings.
   B. He ordered them to shred all of the records about the camp.
   C. He ordered them to eat all of the remaining food.
   D. He ordered them to clean the block.

10. What was the weather like during the evacuation?
    A. It rained the entire time.
    B. It snowed the entire time.
    C. It was clear but below zero.
    D. There was a hail storm.

Sections 6, 7, 8, 9, Pages 81-109

1. While running, an idea began to fascinate Elie. What was the idea?
    A. It was death.
    B. It was escape.
    C. It was murdering the soldiers.
    D. It was finding his mother

2. What did Elie realize about Rabbi Eliahou's son just after the evacuation?
    A. The son was dead and the Rabbi could not admit it.
    B. The son had been trying to lose his father as the men were all running.
    C. The son had escaped and did not take his father.
    D. The son betrayed his father to get extra bread for himself.

3. True or False: Juliek played a Mozart concerto for the men in the camp.
    A. True
    B. False

4. True or False: They were at Gleiwitz for three days. Then they traveled by train for ten days until they reached Buchenwald. A. True
    B. False

5. Who died in the train just before the men were unloaded?
    A. Juliek
    B. Meir Katz
    C. Ezra Malik
    D. Tzipora

6. How many men started out in the train? How many were left when they arrived at Buchenwald?
    A. Ten thousand men started out. Five hundred were left.
    B. Three hundred started out. Fifty were left.
    C. Four thousand started out. Two thousand were left.
    D. One hundred men started out. About twelve were left.

7. What happened to Mr. Wiesel, Elie's father?
    A. He survived.
    B. He died.

8. What was Elie's only desire?
	A. He wanted to eat.
	B. He wanted to sleep.
	C. He wanted to find out if his mother and sisters were alive.
	D. He wanted to take a bath.

9. When did the first American troops arrive at the camp?
	A. 3 AM, May 5, 1946
	B. Midnight, June 1, 1945
	C. 6 PM, April 10, 1945
	D. 10 AM, March 30, 1947

ANSWER KEY-MULTIPLE CHOICE/QUIZ QUESTIONS Night

Section 1, pages 1-20
1. C
2. A
3. D
4. B
5. B FALSE
6. D
7. C, D, B, A
8. B
9. B FALSE

Sections 2, 3, pages 21-43
1. C
2. B
3. A TRUE
4. C
5. C
6. D
7. A
8. A TRUE
9. B FALSE
10. D

Section 4, pages 45-62
1. B FALSE
2. A
3. C
4. A TRUE
5. D
6. B FALSE
7. C
8. C

Section 5, pages 63-80
1. A
2. A TRUE
3. B
4. C
5. A
6. B
7. D
8. C
9. D
10. B

Sections 6,7,8,9. pages 81-109
1. A
2. B
3. B FALSE
4. A TRUE
5. B
6. D
7. B
8. A
9. C

PREREADING VOCABULARY WORKSHEETS

This page is left blank for two-sided printing.

VOCABULARY WORKSHEETS *Night*

<u>Section 1, Pages 1-20</u>

<u>Part I: Using Prior Knowledge and Context Clues</u>
Below are the sentences in which the vocabulary words appear in the text. Read the sentence. Use any clues you can find in the sentence combined with your prior knowledge, and write what you think the underlined words mean on the lines provided.

1. They called him Moshe the Beadle, as though he had never had a **_surname_** in his life.
   _____

2. Nobody ever felt embarrassed by him. Nobody ever felt **_encumbered_** by his presence.
   _____

3. He was a past master in the art of making himself **_insignificant,_** of seeming invisible.
   _____

4. I was twelve. I believed **_profoundly_**. During the day I studied the Talmud, and at night I ran to the synagogue to weep over the destruction of the Temple.
   _____

5. The train full of **_deportees_** had crossed the Hungarian frontier and on Polish territory had been taken in charge by the Gestapo.
   _____

6. At that time, it was still possible to obtain **_emigration_** permits for Palestine.
   _____

7. With some of my schoolmates, I sat in the Ezra Malik gardens, studying a **_treatise_** on the Talmud.
   _____

8. My father was telling them **_anecdotes_** and expounding his own views on the situation.
   _____

9. At dawn, there was nothing left of this **_melancholy_**.
   _____

Night Section 1, Part II: Determining the Meaning

Match the vocabulary words to their dictionary definitions.

_____ 1. surname   A. hindered; restricted
_____ 2. encumbered   B. absolutely; in an unqualified way
_____ 3. insignificant   C. short, humorous stories
_____ 4. profoundly   D. leaving one area to settle in another
_____ 5. deportees   E. sadness; depression
_____ 6. emigration   F. written discussion of a topic
_____ 7. treatise   G. a family name
_____ 8. anecdotes   H. people who are expelled from a country
_____ 9. melancholy   I. trivial; not important

Night Vocabulary: Sections 2, 3, Pages 21-43

Part I: Using Prior Knowledge and Context Clues
Below are the sentences in which the vocabulary words appear in the text. Read the sentence. Use any clues you can find in the sentence combined with your prior knowledge, and write what you think the underlined words mean on the lines provided.

1. Free from all social ***constraint,*** young people gave way openly to instinct, taking advantage of the darkness to flirt in our midst. . .
   _____

2. We still had a few ***provisions*** left. But we never ate enough to satisfy our hunger.
   _____

3. The world was a cattle wagon ***hermetically*** sealed.
   _____

4. The heat, the thirst, the ***pestilential*** stench, the suffocating lack of air-- these were nothing as compared with these screams which tore us to shreds.
   _____

5. In the middle stood the ***notorious*** Dr. Mengele. . .
   _____

6. . . . a typical SS officer: a cruel face, but not ***devoid*** of intelligence, and wearing a monocle.
   _____

7. . . . a typical SS officer: a cruel face, but not devoid of intelligence, and wearing a ***monocle***.
   _____

8. In one ultimate moment of ***lucidity*** it seemed to me that we were damned souls . . .
   _____

9. "You are at Auschwitz. And Auschwitz is not a ***convalescent*** home."
   _____

10. They were all laughing and joking and shouting ***blandishments*** at one another for a good part of the way.
    _____

Night Sections 2-3 Vocabulary Part II: Determining the Meaning

Match the vocabulary words to their dictionary definitions.

_____ 1. constraint   A. necessary supplies, such as food
_____ 2. provisions   B. coaxing by flattery
_____ 3. hermetically   C. clear understanding
_____ 4. pestilential   D. known widely and unfavorably; infamous
_____ 5. notorious   E. restrictions
_____ 6. devoid   F. an eyeglass for one eye
_____ 7. monocle   G. likely to cause an epidemic disease
_____ 8. lucidity   H. completely lacking or empty
_____ 9. convalescent   I. returning to health after an illness
_____10. blandishments   J. sealed against the entry or escape of air

Night Vocabulary: Section 4, Pages 45-62

Part I: Using Prior Knowledge and Context Clues
Below are the sentences in which the vocabulary words appear in the text. Read the sentence. Use any clues you can find in the sentence combined with your prior knowledge, and write what you think the underlined words mean on the lines provided.

1. Our **_convoy_** included a few children ten and twelve years old.
   _____

2. One day when Idek was seized with one of his fits of **_frenzy,_** I got in his way.
   _____

3. This was Franek's chance to **_torment_** my father and to thrash him savagely every day.
   _____

4. This was Franek's chance to torment my father and to **_thrash_** him savagely every day.
   _____

5. I once saw one of thirteen beating his father because the **_latter_** had not made his bed properly.
   _____

6. "Bare your heads!" yelled the head of the camp. His voice was **_raucous_**.
   _____

7. The Gestapo, summoned to the spot, suspected **_sabotage_**. They found a trail.
   _____

Part II: Determining the Meaning
Match the vocabulary words to their dictionary definitions.

_____ 1. convoy   A. boisterous and disorderly
_____ 2. frenzy   B. a group of vehicles traveling together
_____ 3. torment   C. treacherous action to defeat a cause
_____ 4. thrash   D. to cause physical pain or mental anguish
_____ 5. latter   E. second of two
_____ 6. raucous   F. violent mental agitation or wild excitement
_____ 7. sabotage   G. beat; hit

Night Vocabulary: Section 5, Pages 63-80

Part I: Using Prior Knowledge and Context Clues
Below are the sentences in which the vocabulary words appear in the text. Read the sentence. Use any clues you can find in the sentence combined with your prior knowledge, and write what you think the underlined words mean on the lines provided.

1. This day I had ceased to plead. I was no longer capable of ***lamentation***.
   _____

2. In the depths of my heart, I felt a great ***void.***
   _____

3. A poor, ***emaciated***, dried-up Jew questioned him avidly in a trembling voice. . .
   _____

4. Several days had ***elapsed***.
   _____

5. It was a somewhat ***feeble*** argument.
   _____

6. They were quite simply liberated by the Russians two days after the ***evacuation.***
   _____

7. It snowed ***relentlessly.***
   _____

Part II: Determining the Meaning
Match the vocabulary words to their dictionary definitions.

　　_____ 1. lamentation　　　A. grief; mourning
　　_____ 2. void　　　　　　 B. steadily; persistently
　　_____ 3. emaciated　　　　C. made thin due to starvation
　　_____ 4. elapsed　　　　　D. withdrawing troops or civilians
　　_____ 5. feeble　　　　　 E. passed
　　_____ 6. evacuation　　　 F. lacking strength, weak
　　_____ 7. relentlessly　　 G. emptiness

Night Vocabulary: Sections 6, 7, 8, 9, Pages 81-109

Part I: Using Prior Knowledge and Context Clues
Below are the sentences in which the vocabulary words appear in the text. Read the sentence. Use any clues you can find in the sentence combined with your prior knowledge, and write what you think the underlined words mean on the lines provided.

1. Their fingers on the triggers, they did not ***deprive*** themselves of this pleasure.
   _____

2. He sat up and looked round him, bewildered, stupefied--a ***bereaved*** stare.
   _____

3. From time to time, the SS officers on motorcycles would go down the length of the column to try and shake us out of our growing ***apathy***.
   _____

4. His ***livid*** face was covered with a layer of frost.
   _____

5. The days were like nights, and the nights left the ***dregs*** of their darkness in our souls.
   _____

6. Wild beasts of prey, with animal hatred in their eyes; an extraordinary ***vitality*** had seized them, sharpening their teeth and nails.
   _____

7. He was finished, at the end of his ***tether***.
   _____

8. The ***contagion*** spread to the other carriages.
   _____

9. A ***plaintive***, beseeching voice caught me in the spine.
   _____

10. And, in the depths of my being, in the ***recesses*** of my weakened conscience, could I have searched it, I might perhaps have found something like--free at last!
    _____

Night Sections 6-9 Vocabulary Part II: Determining the Meaning

Match the vocabulary words to their dictionary definitions.

_____ 1. deprive   A. lack of emotion or feeling
_____ 2. bereaved   B. ashen; pallid
_____ 3. apathy   C. harmful influence
_____ 4. livid   D. expressing sorrow
_____ 5. dregs   E. the least desirable portions
_____ 6. vitality   F. the limit of one's resources or endurance
_____ 7. tether   G. remote, secret places
_____ 8. contagion   H. vigor; energy
_____ 9. plaintive   I. left alone by death
_____10. recesses   J. to take something away from

ANSWER KEY-PREREADING VOCABULARY WORKSHEETS
Night

Section 1
1. G
2. A
3. I
4. B
5. H
6. D
7. F
8. C
9. E

Sections 2, 3
1. E
2. A
3. J
4. G
5. D
6. H
7. F
8. C
9. I
10. B

Section 4
1. B
2. F
3. D
4. G
5. E
6. A
7. C

Section 5
1. A
2. G
3. C
4. E
5. F
6. D
7. B

Sections 6, 7, 8, 9
1. J
2. I
3. A
4. B
5. E
6. H
7. F
8. C
9. D
10. G

DAILY LESSONS

This page is left blank for two-sided printing.

LESSON ONE

Student Objectives
1. To develop research skills
2. To write to inform by developing and organizing facts to convey information
3. To complete Writing Assignment #1 and the Nonfiction assignment

Activity
   Assign one of the following topics (or topics of your choice) to each of the students. Distribute Writing Assignment #1 and the Nonfiction Assignment sheet and discuss them. Students should fill this out the Nonfiction Assignment sheet for at least one of the sources they used and submit it along with their report. Take students to the library for the rest of the period to work on the assignment.

Topics
1. Make a time line of World War II.

2. Research the country of Transylvania. Include its location on a map of prewar Europe.

3. Name the Allies and Axis countries and their leaders. Summarize the political policies and philosophies of each.

4. Identify Adolph Hitler and his role in the Third Reich.

5. Trace the persecution of the Jewish people in Europe.

6. Research the Jewish faith. Include major beliefs and holy days.

7. Explain the beliefs and practices of the Hasidic Jews. Compare these to the beliefs and practices of the Reform Jews.

8. Trace the origin and development of the Jewish nation.

9. Briefly explain the teachings of the Talmud, the Zohar and the cabbala.

10. Obtain information on the Holocaust from the Holocaust Museum in Washington, DC, or another source.

11. Describe any one of the concentration camps. Include a map with its location.

Night Nonfiction Topics Continued:

12. Describe the Occupation. Include the events that led up to it.

13. Describe the countries that made up pre-war Europe. Include the racial make-up of each. Draw a map to show the location of each country.

14. Discuss the involvement of the United States in World War II.

15. Summarize the events of World War I and explain how they led to World War II.

16. Explain the roles of the SS and the Gestapo.

17. Explain the significance of the Nobel Peace Prize.

18. Read and report on Elie Wiesel's continuing work for peace and human rights.

19. Explain how and where the surviving Jewish people resettled after the war.

WRITING ASSIGNMENT #1 *Night*
Writing to Inform

PROMPT
You are reading about the events that took place in the life of one teen-aged boy, Elie Wiesel. The setting for the autobiographical sketch is Europe in the years between 1941 and 1945. I order to better understand the terrible things that happened to him and millions of other people, you must first understand what the world was like at that time.

PREWRITING
Your teacher may assign a topic or allow you to choose one. You will then go to the library to research the topic. Look for encyclopedias, books, magazine articles, videos, and Internet sources. You may want to interview an expert on the topic of your choice.

Think of questions you have about your topic. Write each one on a separate index card. Then read to find the answers, and write them on the cards. Also take notes on interesting and important facts, even if you did not have questions about them. Put each fact on a separate card. Make sure to cite your references. That means to write down the title of the book or article, the author, and the page number for each one.

Arrange your note card in the order you want to use for your paper. Number them, perhaps in the upper right hand corner. Read through them to make sure they make sense in that order. Rearrange as necessary.

DRAFTING
Introduce your topic in the first paragraph. Tell why you chose it, and give a preview of what the rest of the paper will be about. Then write several paragraphs about the topic. Each paragraph should have a main idea and supporting details. Your last paragraph should summarize the information in the report.

PEER CONFERENCE/REVISING
When you finish the rough draft, ask another student to look at it. You may want to give the student your note cards so he/she can double check for you and see that you have included all of the information. After reading, he or she should tell you what he/she liked best about your report, which parts were difficult to understand or needed more information, and ways in which your work could be improved. Reread your report considering your critic's comments and make the corrections you think are necessary.

PROOFREADING/EDITING
Do a final proofreading of your report, double-checking your grammar, spelling, organization, and the clarity of your ideas.

WRITING EVALUATION FORM *Night*

Name _____ Date _____ Class _____

Writing Assignment # _____

Circle One For Each Item:

Composition	excellent	good	fair	poor
Style	excellent	good	fair	poor
Grammar	excellent	good	fair	poor
Spelling	excellent	good	fair	poor
Punctuation	excellent	good	fair	poor
Legibility	excellent	good	fair	poor

Strengths:

Weaknesses:

Comments/Suggestions:

NONFICTION ASSIGNMENT SHEET *Night* (To be completed after reading the required nonfiction article)

Name _____ Date _____ Class/ _____

Title of Nonfiction Read _____

Author _____ Publication Date _____

I. **Factual Summary:** Write a short summary of the piece you read.

II. **Vocabulary:**
   1. Which vocabulary words were difficult?

   2. What did you do to help yourself understand the words?

III. **Interpretation:** What was the main point the author wanted you to get from reading his/her work?

IV. **Criticism:**
   1. Which points of the piece did you agree with or find easy to believe? Why?

   2. With which points of the piece did you disagree or find difficult to believe? Why?

V. **Personal Response:**
   1. What do you think about this piece?

   2. How does this piece help you better understand the novel *Night?*

LESSON TWO

Student Objectives
    1. To continue doing library research for the nonfiction assignment
    2. To write to inform

Activity #1
    Either take the students to the library or give them time in class to work on their research projects.

Activity #2
    While the writing conferences are scheduled for Lesson Three, you may want to begin them during Lesson Two if some of the students are ready. Establish a quiet section of the room for the conferences.

LESSON THREE

Student Objectives
    1. To participate in a writing conference with the teacher
    2. To revise the nonfiction assignment based on the suggestions made during the writing conference

Activity #1
    Choose a quiet location in the room to hold the writing conferences.

Activity #2
    Students should be working independently on their research projects when they are not conferencing.

LESSON FOUR

<u>Objectives</u>
1. To widen the breadth of students' knowledge about the topics discussed or touched upon in *Night*
2. To check students' non-fiction assignments

<u>Activity</u>

Ask each student to give a brief oral report about the nonfiction work he/she read for the nonfiction assignment. Your criteria for evaluating this report will vary depending on the level of your students. You may wish for students to give a complete report without using notes of any kind, or you may want students to read directly from a written report, or you may want to do something in between these two extremes. Just make students aware of your criteria in ample time for them to prepare their reports.

Start with one student's report. After that, ask if anyone else in the class has read on a topic related to the first student's report. If no one has, choose another student at random. After each report, be sure to ask if anyone has a report related to the one just completed. That will help keep a continuity during the discussion of the reports.

LESSON FIVE

Student Objectives
1. To preview the *Night* Unit
2. To receive books and other related materials (study guides, reading assignment)
3. To relate prior knowledge to the new material
4. To become familiar with the vocabulary for Section 1
5. To preview the study questions for Chapters Section 1
6. To read Section 1

Activity #1

Distribute the materials students will use in this unit. Explain in detail how students are to use these materials.

Study Guides Students should preview the study guide questions before each reading assignment to get a feeling for what events and ideas are important in that section. After reading the section, students will (as a class or individually) answer the questions to review the important events and ideas from that section of the book. Students should keep the study guides as study materials for the unit test.

Reading Assignment Sheet You need to fill in the reading assignment sheet to let students know when their reading has to be completed. You can either write the assignment sheet on a side blackboard or bulletin board and leave it there for students to see each day, or you can duplicate copies for each student to have. In either case, you should advise students to become very familiar with the reading assignments so they know what is expected of them.

Unit Outline You may find it helpful to distribute copies of the Unit Outline to your students so they can keep track of upcoming lessons and assignments. You may also want to post a copy of the Unit Outline on a bulletin board and cross off each lesson as you complete it.

Extra Activities Center The resource portions of this unit contains suggestions for a library of related books and articles in your classroom as well as crossword and word search puzzles. Make an extra activities center in your room where you will keep these materials for students to use. Bring the books and articles in from the library and keep several copies of the puzzles on hand. Explain to students that these materials are available for students to use when they finish reading assignments or other class work early.

Books Each school has its own rules and regulations regarding student use of school books. Advise students of the procedures that are normal for your school.

Notebook or Unit Folder You may want the students to keep all of their worksheets, notes, and other papers for the unit together in a binder or notebook. During the first class meeting, tell them how you want them to arrange the folder. Make divider pages for vocabulary worksheets, prereading study guide questions, review activities, notes, and tests. You may want to give a grade for accuracy in keeping the folder.

Activity #2

Do a group KWL Sheet with the students (form included.) Students should know something about the Holocaust after completing the research projects, and will have information to share. Put this information in the K column (What I Know.) Ask students what they want to find out from reading *Night* and record this in the W column (What I Want to Find Out.) Keep the sheet and refer back to it after reading the book. Complete the L column (What I Learned) at that time.

Activity #4

Work through the prereading vocabulary worksheet for Section 1 with the students. Tell them they will have a sheet like this to complete before reading each section of the book.

Activity #5

Show students how to preview the study questions for Section 1 of *Night*. Encourage students to predict what they think answers might be, to write down their predictions, and to compare these with their answers after reading the chapters.

Activity #6

Begin reading Section 1 aloud to the class. Invite willing students to continue reading aloud until the end of the class period. Tell students to complete the reading before the next class meeting.

KWL *Night*

Directions: Before reading, think about what you already know about *Night* and/or Elie Wiesel. Write the information in the K column. Think about what you would like to find out from reading the book. Write your questions in the W column. After you have read the book, use the L column to write the answers to your questions from the W column, and anything else you remember from the book.

What I Know	What I Want to Find Out	What I Learned

LESSON SIX

<u>Student Objectives</u>
1. To review the main ideas and themes in Section 1
2. To discuss the mood and tone of the book
3. To begin Writing Assignment #2

<u>Activity #1</u>

Discuss the answers to the Study Guide questions for Section 1 in detail. Write the answers on the board or overhead projector so students can have the correct answers for study purposes. Encourage students to take notes. If the students own their books, encourage them to use high lighter pens to mark important passages and the answers to the study guide questions.

Note: It is a good practice in public speaking and leadership skills for individual students to take charge of leading the discussion of the study questions. Perhaps a different student could go to the front of the class and lead the discussion each day that the study questions are discussed during this unit. Of course, the teacher should guide the discussion when appropriate and be sure to fill in any gaps the students leave.

<u>Activity #2 Minilesson: Mood</u>

The mood or tone of a story is the author's attempt to create the atmosphere of story. The mood evokes an emotional response from the reader and lets the reader know how the characters feel. It may stay the same throughout a story, or it may changed, depending on circumstances and events. The author's descriptions and the characters' dialogue and actions express the mood of the story. Mood can be stated or implied.

Ask the students to give their impressions of the mood conveyed by the title and jacket artwork. Have them reread the first section of the book to see where and how the mood changes from relatively pleasant to fearful. Make a list of words that Wiesel uses to invoke a certain mood. You may want to keep this as a chart or bulletin board that students can add to throughout the unit. Tell students to keep the mood of the book in mind as they read. They will have the opportunity to discuss mood again during Lesson Thirteen.

Activity #3 (Writing Assignment #2)

Tell students they will be keeping a sketchbook-journal as Writing Assignment #2. Explain that a sketchbook-journal is a combination of sketches about and written responses to the story. They will be required to make an entry for each chapter in the novel.

Students can sketch memorable scenes from the chapters, or paste in magazine pictures that remind them of the events in the chapter.

The written entries should focus on each student's response to the literature, and should not merely be a plot summary. They should include comments about their thoughts and feelings while reading, any questions they have, and predictions for the next chapter. For *Night*, encourage them to write about the mood of the story.

It is up to the individual teacher to decide how to grade or respond to the journals, and whether to have students share them with the class or keep them private.

WRITING ASSIGNMENT #2 *Night*
Journal Writing to Express a Personal Opinion

PROMPT

    For this unit, you will be asked to keep a sketchbook-journal. This is a combination of sketches about and written responses to a story. You will be required to make an entry for each chapter in the novel.

    First, decide on the format for your sketchbook-journal. Spend some time decorating your cover and setting up the book. Make sure to include the title of each chapter and the page numbers in you copy of the book. Also date each entry.

    You can sketch memorable scenes from the chapters, paste in magazine pictures, or use computer clip art.. Even if you do not consider yourself a good artist, try to make some sketches. Use colors that remind you of the mood of the story. You may want to take photographs and put them in the sketchbook-journal.

    The written entries should focus on your response to the literature, and should not merely be chapter summaries. They should include comments about your thoughts and feelings while reading, any questions you have, and predictions about the next chapter. Try to write at least one page for each entry. You, your class mates and your teacher will decide whether to share the journals or keep them private.

    Here are some suggestions for the types of entries you may want to make.

Check Your Understanding	Explain how the story is making sense to you. Give examples and note page numbers. Establish the setting, mood, point of view, and character-relationships. Discuss the stated themes.
Make Inferences	Explain your thoughts about the feelings and motives of the characters. Discuss the implied themes.
Make and Revise Predictions	At the end of each chapter, make a prediction about what you think will happen next. After you read, go back and check your predictions. Tell if you had to revise them, and why.
Ask Questions	Ask questions about scenes or events that are confusing. Record the answers if you discuss the questions in class, or later find the answer in the novel.

Give Your Opinion	Give your opinion about the literary quality of the work. Discuss the author's style, use of language, and use of literary devices. Tell why you do nor do not like the story. Tell how you feel while reading the chapters. Compare the book with others you have read.
Make Connections	Think about ways the characters and events relate to your own life and experiences. Put yourself in the character's place and discuss how you would think or feel in that situation. Try this from the point of view of the main character and a few of the minor ones.
Make Recommendations	Tell what you think the characters should do or say. Tell how you would end the story, or what you think might happen next.

LESSON SEVEN

Student Objectives
    1. To become familiar with the vocabulary for Sections 2 and 3
    2. To preview the study questions for Sections 2 and 3
    3. To practice correct intonation and expression in oral reading
    4. To read from Sections 2 and 3 orally for evaluation

Activity #1
    Give students ten or fifteen minutes to complete the prereading vocabulary worksheet and preview the study questions.

Activity #2
    Tell students their oral reading ability will be evaluated. Show them copies of the Oral Reading Evaluation Form and discuss it. Model correct intonation and expression by reading the first few paragraphs of Section 2 aloud.

Activity #3
    Call on individual students to read a few paragraphs aloud. Encourage the other students to follow along silently in their books. If you have a student who is unwilling or unable to read in front of the group make arrangements to do his or her evaluation privately at another time.

Activity #4
    Tell students to have answers for the study questions prepared for the next class meeting.

ORAL READING EVALUATION *Night*

Name _____   Class _____ Date _____

Page or pages read: _____

SKILL	EXCELLENT	GOOD	AVERAGE	FAIR	POOR
FLUENCY	5	4	3	2	1
CLARITY	5	4	3	2	1
AUDIBILITY	5	4	3	2	1
PRONUNCIATION	5	4	3	2	1
_____	5	4	3	2	1
_____	5	4	3	2	1

TOTAL _____   **GRADE** _____

COMMENTS:

LESSON EIGHT

Student Objectives
    1. To discuss the main ideas and events in Sections 2 and 3
    2. To become familiar with the vocabulary for Section 4
    3. To preview the study questions for Section 4
    4. To identify the types of conflict in the novel
    5. To read Section 4

Activity #1
    Give each student four 1"x2" strips of colored paper or index cards--one blue, one yellow, one green, one pink. Have them put a large letter A on the blue paper, B on the yellow, C on the green, and D on the pink. Make an overhead transparency of the Multiple Choice/Quiz questions for Sections 2 and 3. Ask a student to read the first question out loud. Have each student hold up the colored paper strip for their answer. Encourage students to reread if necessary to find the correct answers.

Activity #2
    Have students work with partners to complete the prereading vocabulary worksheet and preview the study questions.

Activity #3
    Activity #2 Minilesson: Conflict
    Tell students that conflict is one of the most important aspects of a story. The conflict usually is an obstacle to the main character's goal. It usually brings about some type of change in the main character. The types of conflict that are evident in *Night* are character vs. nature, character vs. character, character vs. himself, and character vs. society.
    You may want to use examples from stories the students have previously read, or examples from literature for younger children to illustrate the various types of conflict. Dorothy in *The Wizard of Oz* has a conflict with nature because the tornado takes her away from her home. The conflict between Cinderella and her wicked step-mother is an example of character vs. character. In *The Little Engine That Could*, the little engine is not sure of its ability to take the train over the mountain, illustrating the character vs. himself conflict. The Greek myth of Atalanta illustrates character vs. society or the environment. Atalanta was expected to marry the man her father chose, but she did not wish to do so. Have students begin filling out the Conflict Chart after they have read Section 3. Discuss their findings. Encourage them to look for more examples of conflict as they read. Tell them they will discuss conflict again in Lesson Thirteen.

CONFLICT CHART *Night*

Directions: Use the chart below to record examples of the different types of conflict you read about in *Night*

CONFLICT	EXAMPLE and PAGES	CHANGE in Elie
CHARACTER VS. NATURE		
CHARACTER VS. SELF		
CHARACTER VS. SOCIETY		
CHARACTER VS. CHARACTER		

LESSON NINE

Student Objectives
1. To review the main events and ideas of Section 4
2. To identify examples of figurative language in the story so far
2. To become familiar with the vocabulary for Section 5
3. To preview the study questions for Section 5

Activity #1
Review the study questions for Section 4 to review the important events and ideas in Section 4.

Activity #2 Minilesson: Figures of Speech
Figures of speech are literary devices that give the writer a non-literal way to describe images and events. Use the following chart to give examples of the different figures of speech. (You may want to make an overhead transparency, or duplicate the chart for each student.) Then write *physically he was as awkward as a clown* on the board. (This is Elie Wiesel's description of Moshe the Beadle on page 1 of the book.) Ask students to identify the type of figure of speech (simile.) Talk about the literal meaning. Distribute the Figure of Speech worksheet and have students work in small groups to find examples in the novel. If you want the students to continue recording examples in the remaining chapters, assign a due date for the worksheet.

Activity #3
Give students about ten or fifteen minutes to complete the prereading vocabulary worksheets and preview the study questions for Section 5.

LESSON TEN

Student Objectives
1. To read Section 5 with a partner
2. To discuss the main ideas and events in Section 5

Activity #1
Assign or let students choose partners. Have them read Section 5 aloud together quietly.

Activity #2
Divide students into ten groups. Assign each group one of the study questions to research and answer for the class.

FIGURES OF SPEECH *Night*

Figures of speech are literary devices that give the writer a non-literal way to describe images and events. They are comparisons that help the reader create a mental image of a character or a situation.

HYPERBOLE	Extreme exaggeration used to describe a person or thing. For example: *She has as many pairs of earrings as there are stars in the sky.*
IRONY	The use of words to express something different from and often opposite to their literal meaning. For example: *Yeah, being a kid is one laugh after another.*
METAPHOR	A comparison without the words **like** or **as**. For example: *The cat is a bag of bones.*
METONYMY	A figure of speech in which one word or phrase is substituted for another with which it is closely associated, as in the use of *Washington* for the United States government or of *the sword* for military power.
ONOMATOPOEIA	The use of words such as *buzz* or *splash* that imitate the sounds associated with the objects or actions they refer to.
PARADOX	A seemingly self-contradictory statement that has some truth to it. For example: *sitting may be more exhausting than standing*
PERSONIFICATION	Attributing human characteristics to inanimate objects, animals, or ideas, as in *the wind howled.*
SIMILE	A comparison using the words **like** or **as**. For example: *I felt as light as a feather.*

FIGURES OF SPEECH *Night*

Figures of speech are literary devices that give the writer a non-literal way to describe images and events. The main types of figures of speech are hyperbole, irony, metaphor, metonymy, onomatopoeia, paradox, personification, and simile. Use the following chart to record examples of figures of speech used in *Night*. A sample has been done for you. Note: You may not find an example of each figure of speech in the novel.

Figure of Speech	Example from Novel, page #	Literal Meaning
simile	*physically he was as awkward as a clown*	He was clumsy and not graceful.

LESSON ELEVEN

Student Objectives
    1. To become familiar with the vocabulary for Sections 6-9
    2. To preview the study questions for Sections 6-9
    3. To read Sections 6-9

Activity #1
    Give students about ten minutes to complete the prereading vocabulary worksheet.

Activity #2
    Distribute copies of the multiple choice study questions for Sections 6-9. Have students circle their predicted answers before reading the text. Then make the reading assignment for Sections 6-9, which should be completed prior to the next class meeting.

LESSON TWELVE

Student Objectives
    1. To discuss the main ideas and events in Sections 6-9
    2. To chronicle the events sequentially

Activity #1
    Go over the answers to the multiple choice study questions. Use the short answer questions as well if you want to get into more detail about the events concerning Juliek, Meir Katz, and the death of Elie Wiesel's father.

Activity #2 Minilesson: Sequence
    In an autobiographical sketch such as *Night*, the sequence of events is very important. Since so many dates are given, it is relatively easy to follow the sequence of events in *Night*. Use a roll of shelf or art paper to make a large time line of the events in the book. For advanced students, assign each section of the book to a small group. Have the group write each important event on an index card and paste it in the correct place on the time line. For average classes, work with the whole class and guide them in finding and recording the major events. For students who need extra assistance, make up cards with the major dates and events listed, one per card. Distribute the cards to the students and have them put the cards in order on the class time line. Show them how to skim and reread to find the dates and events in the book. Encourage students to make illustrations to go with the time line.

LESSON THIRTEEN

Student Objective
   To discuss *Night* at the interpretive and critical levels

Activity #1
   Choose the questions from the Extra Writing Assignments/Discussion Questions which seem most appropriate for your students. A class discussion of these questions is most effective if students have been given the opportunity to formulate answers to the questions prior to the discussion. To this end, you may either have all the students formulate answers to all the questions, divide the class into groups and assign one or more questions to each group, or you could assign one question to each student in your class. The option you choose will make a difference in the amount of class time needed for this activity.

Activity #2
   After students have had ample time to formulate answers to the questions, begin your class discussion of the questions and the ideas presented by the questions. Be sure students take notes during the discussion so they have information to study for the unit test.

LESSON FOURTEEN

Student Objective
   To write a persuasive essay

Activity #1
   Distribute copies of Writing Assignment #3. Discuss it in detail and make sure the students understand what to do.

Activity #2
   Allow the rest of the class period for students to work on the assignment.

Option
   You may want to let students work with a partner or a small group for this assignment. If so, make sure they understand that they will receive the same grade.

Activity #3
   If time permits, invite students to role play and give their persuasive speeches in class.

EXTRA WRITING ASSIGNMENT/DISCUSSION QUESTIONS *Night*

<u>Interpretation</u>

1. From what point of view is the story written? How does this affect our understanding of the story?

2. Why didn't the townspeople listen to Moshe the Beadle?

3. Describe Elie's relationship with Moshe the Beadle.

4. Why did the young girl at Buna risk her safety to speak to Elie in German?

5. In Section 4, Wiesel described the hanging of one young man. Then he said his soup was excellent that evening. What did he mean?

6. In Section 4, Wiesel described the hanging of the *pipel*, the young servant boy. He said the soup tasted of corpses that night. What did he mean?

7. Describe and analyze Elie Wiesel's changing view of God throughout the book.

8. In Section 6, why did Mr. Wiesel smile?

9. Describe the relationship between Elie and his father while they were in the concentration camps. Compare and contrast this with their relationship before their imprisonment.

10. Why do you think Moshe the Beadle stayed in Singhet when the people would not listen to him? What does this say about his character?

11. Why do you think Mr. Wiesel refused to go with Martha when she offered a safe refuge?

12. Was Madame Schächter crazy, or was she able to predict what was going to happen to the Jews?

13. Why did the Jews hold onto their illusions for so long?

14. In Section 5, why did Elie and his father choose to be evacuated instead of staying in the hospital?

Critical
15. How did Elie Wiesel change over the course of the book? Were these changes for the better?

16. The author often used vivid language to describe a scene or event. Give an example of his use of vivid language that you found most effective. Tell why it was effective.

17. What was the overall mood of the story? Give examples to support your answer.

18. How would the story change if there were a different narrator?

19. Which character do you know the most about? Which character do you know the least about?

20. Were you able to predict the ending? What clues did the author give?

21. Discuss the author's use of language. Is it natural? Do people you know talk the way the characters did?

22. Does the mood of the story change? How does the author show this?

23. What words does the author use to create the atmosphere of the book?

24. Were the descriptions in the book effective? Give some examples.

25. Which senses did the descriptions cause you to use? Give examples of the descriptions using hearing, seeing, touching, smelling, taste.

Personal Response
26. Did you enjoy reading *Night?* Why or why not?

27. Is *Night* a good title for the book? Why or why not? If not, what title would you suggest?

28. Did you have strong feelings while reading this book? If so, what did the author do to cause those feelings? If not, why not?

29. Will you read more of Elie Wiesel's books? Why or why not?

30. Did Elie Wiesel's experiences change the way you look at yourself? How?

31. Have you read any other stories similar to *Night* ? If so, tell about them.

32. Would you recommend this book to another student? Why or why not?

33. What makes Elie Wiesel a unique and different author?

34. What questions would you like to ask Elie Wiesel?

35. What was the saddest part of the story?

36. What do you remember most about the story?

37. What picture did the author leave in your mind?

38. What did the book make you think about?

QUOTATIONS *Night*

1. "Man raises himself toward God by the questions he asks Him," he was fond of repeating. "That is the true dialogue. Man questions God and God answers. But we don't understand His answers. We can't understand them. Because they come from the depths of the soul and they stay there until death. You will find the true answers, Eliezer, only within yourself!"

2. "Jews, listen to me. It's all I ask of you. I don't want money or pity. Only listen to me."

3. "You don't understand," he said in despair. "You can't understand. I have been saved miraculously. I managed to get back here. Where did I get the strength from? I wanted to come back to Singhet to tell you the story of my death, so that you could prepare yourselves while there was still time. To live? I don't attach any importance to my life any more. I'm alone. No, I wanted to come back, and to warn you. And see how it is, no one will listen to me."

4. People said, "The Russian army's making gigantic strides forward. . . . Hitler won't be able to do us any harm, even if he wants to."

5. "The yellow star? Oh, well, what of it? You don't die of it . . . ."

6. "Get up, sir, get up! You've got to get ready for the journey! You're going to be expelled from here tomorrow with your whole family, and all the rest of the Jews. Where to? Don't ask me, sir. Don't ask me any questions. Only God could answer you. For heaven's sake, get up."

7. "Oh, God, Lord of the Universe, take pity upon us in Thy great mercy. . . . "

8. "You can go if you want to. I shall stay here with your mother and the child."

9. "Who knows? Perhaps we are being deported for our own good. The front isn't very far off; we shall soon be able to hear the guns. And then the civilian population would be evacuated anyway. . . . "

10. "Look! Look at it! Fire! A terrible fire! Mercy! *Oh, that fire!* Jews, listen to me! I can see a fire! There are huge flames! It is a furnace!"

11. "Men to the left! Women to the right!"

12. "No, not fifty. Forty. Do you understand? Eighteen and forty."

13. "Let the world learn of the existence of Auschwitz. Let everybody hear about it, while they can still escape. . . . "

14. "Humanity? Humanity is not concerned with us. Today anything is allowed. Anything is possible, even these crematories."

15. "Remember this. Remember it forever. Engrave it into your minds. You are at Auschwitz. And Auschwitz is not a convalescent home. It's a concentration camp. Here, you have got to work. If not, you will go straight to the furnace. To the crematory. Work or the crematory--the choice is in your hands."

16. "Bite your lip, little brother. . . . don't cry. Keep your anger and your hatred for another day, for later on. The day will come, but not now. . . . Wait. Grit your teeth and wait."

17. "God is testing us. He wants to find out whether we can dominate our base instincts and kill the Satan within us. We have no right to despair. And if he punishes us relentlessly, it's a sign that He loves us all the more."

18. "Am I Jewish? Yes, I am Jewish. From a religious family. During the occupation I obtained forged papers and passed myself off as an Aryan. That's how I was enlisted in the forced labor groups, and when I was deported to Germany, I escaped the concentration camp. At the warehouse, no one knew I could speak German. That would have aroused suspicions. Saying those few words to you was risky; but I knew you wouldn't give me away."

19. "They're bombing Buna!"

20. "Long live liberty! A curse upon Germany! A curse. . . . A cur--"

21. "Where is He? Here He is--He is hanging here on the gallows."

22. "What are You, my God," I thought angrily, "compared to this afflicted crowd, proclaiming to You their faith, their anger, their revolt? What does Your greatness mean, Lord of the universe, in the face of all this weakness, this decomposition, and this decay? Why do You still trouble their sick minds, their crippled bodies?"

23. "It's the end. God is no longer with us."

24. "I've got more faith in Hitler than in anyone else. He's the only one who's kept his promises, all his promises, to the Jewish people."

25. "Don't think. Don't stop. Run."

26. "Perhaps someone has seen my son somewhere?"

27. "No! He isn't dead! Not yet!"

28. "Why don't they shoot us all right away?"

29. "Listen to me, boy. Don't forget that you're in a concentration camp. Here, every man has to fight for himself and not think of anyone else. Even of his father. Here, there are no fathers, no brothers, no friends. Everyone lives and dies for himself alone. I'll give you a sound piece of advice--don't give your ration of bread and soup to your old father. There's nothing you can do for him. And you're killing yourself. Instead, you ought to be having his ration."

WRITING ASSIGNMENT #3 *Night*
Writing to Persuade

PROMPT

Four times in the novel, Elie Wiesel describes times he and his family might have been saved, had they made a different decision. First, Moshe the Beadle tried to convince the Jews of Singhet to flee from the coming persecution, but no one listened to him. Then, Elie tried to convince his father to sell the business and emigrate to Palestine. Later, the Wiesel family refused the safe refuge offered by their former servant, Martha. When Elie and his father were given the choice to stay at the camp hospital or be evacuated with the other prisoners, they chose to stay with the others. Your assignment is to choose one of these opportunities and convince the Wiesel family to make the opposite decision of the one they made.

PREWRITING

Make a list of the reasons you want the family to leave Singhet, go with Martha, or stay at the hospital. Think of statements to support each of your reasons, and list them under each reason. You can also include reasons you disagree with them. Then number the reasons in order from most to least important.

DRAFTING

Make an introductory statement in which you state the problem (the Wiesel family and the other Jewish residents/prisoners are in grave danger.) Then offer your solution. Use one paragraph for each of your reasons. Use supporting statements for each reason. Include examples, facts, and feelings that support your position. Write a closing paragraph that restates your request and summarizes your arguments.

PEER CONFERENCING/REVISING

When you finish the rough draft, ask another student to look at it. You may want to give the student your notes so he/she can double check for you and see that you have included all of the information. After reading, he or she should tell you what he/she liked best about your persuasive essay, which parts were difficult to understand or needed more information, and ways in which your work could be improved. Reread your persuasive essay considering your critic's comments and make the corrections you think are necessary.

PROOFREADING/EDITING

Do a final proofreading of your persuasive essay, double-checking your grammar, spelling, organization, and the clarity of your ideas.

FINAL DRAFT/PUBLISHING

Complete the final draft according to your teacher's instructions.

LESSON SIXTEEN

Student Objective
 To review all of the vocabulary work done in this unit

VOCABULARY REVIEW ACTIVITIES

1. Divide your class into two teams and have an old-fashioned spelling or definition bee.

2. Give individuals or groups of students a Vocabulary Word Search Puzzle from the Vocabulary Resource section. . The person (group) to find all of the vocabulary words in the puzzle first wins.

3. Give students a Vocabulary Word Search Puzzle without the word list. The person or group to find the most vocabulary words in the puzzle wins.

4. Put a Vocabulary Crossword Puzzle onto a transparency on the overhead projector and do the puzzle together as a class.

5. Give students a Vocabulary Matching, Multiple Choice, or Magic Square worksheet to do.

6. Use words from the word jumble page and have students spell them correctly.

7. Have students write a story in which they correctly use as many vocabulary words as possible. Have students read their compositions orally. Post the most original compositions on your bulletin board.

8. Have students work in teams and play charades with the vocabulary words.

9. Select a word of the day and encourage students to use it correctly in their writing and speaking vocabulary.

10. Have a contest to see which students can find the most vocabulary words used in other sources. You may want to have a bulletin board available so the students can write down their word, the sentence it was used in, and the source.

11. Assign a word to each student, or let them choose a word. Have them look up the origin of the word, the part of speech, definition, a synonym, and an antonym. Then have them write a sentence using the word. Have students present their information orally to the class, or have them design a word map on paper and display the papers.

LESSON SIXTEEN

Objective
    To review the main ideas presented in *Night*

Activity #1
    Choose one of the review games/activities included in the packet and spend your class period as outlined there.

Activity #2
    Remind students of the date for the Unit Test. Stress the review of the Study Guides and their class notes as a last minute, brush-up review for homework.

REVIEW GAMES / ACTIVITIES

1. Ask the class to make up a unit test for *Night*. The test should have 4 sections: multiple choice, true/false, short answer and essay. Students may use 1/2 period to make the test, including a separate answer sheet, and then swap papers and use the other 1/2 class period to take a test a classmate has devised. (open book)

2. Take 1/2 period for students to make up true and false questions (including the answers). Collect the papers and divide the class into two teams. Draw a big tic-tac-toe board on the chalk board. Make one team X and one team O. Ask questions to each side, giving each student one turn. If the question is answered correctly, that student's team's letter (X or O) is placed in the box. If the answer is incorrect, no mark is placed in the box. The object is to get three marks in a row like tic-tac-toe. You may want to keep track of the number of games won for each team.

3. Take 1/2 period for students to make up questions (true/false and short answer). Collect the questions. Divide the class into two teams. You'll alternate asking questions to individual members of teams A & B (like in a spelling bee). The question keeps going from A to B until it is correctly answered, then a new question is asked. A correct answer does not allow the team to get another question. Correct answers are +2 points; incorrect answers are -1 point.

4. Allow students time to quiz each other (in pairs) from their study guides and class notes.

5. Give students a crossword puzzle from the *Night* Unit Resources packet to complete.

7. Divide your class into two teams. Use the crossword words with their letters jumbled as a word list. Student 1 from Team A faces off against Student 1 from Team B. You write the first jumbled word on the board. The first student (1A or 1B) to unscramble the word wins the chance for his/her team to score points. If 1A wins the jumble, go to student 2A and give him/her a clue. He/she must give you the correct word which matches that clue. If he/she does, Team A scores a point, and you give student 3A a clue for which you expect another correct response. Continue giving Team A clues until some team member makes an incorrect response. An incorrect response sends the game back to the jumbled-word face off, this time with students 2A and 2B. Instead of repeating giving clues to the first few students of each team, continue with the student after the one who gave the last incorrect response on the team.

8. Take on the persona of "The Answer Person." Allow students to ask any question about the book. Answer the questions, or tell students where to look in the book to find the answer.

9. Students may enjoy playing charades with events from the story. Select a student to start. Give him/her a card with a scene or event from the story. Allow the players to use their books to find the scene being described. The first person to guess each charade performs the next one.

10. Play a categories-type quiz game. (A master is included in this Unit Plan). Make an overhead transparency of the categories form. Divide the class into teams of three or four players each. Have each team Choose a recorder and a banker. Choose a team to go first. That team will choose a category and point amount. Ask the question to the entire class. (Use the Study Guide Quiz and Vocabulary questions.) Give the teams one minute to discuss the answer and write it down. Walk around the room and check the answers. Each team that answers correctly receives the points. (Incorrect answers are not penalized; they just don't receive any points). Cross out that square on the playing board. Play continues until all squares have been used. The winning team is the one with the most points. You can assign bonus points to any square or squares you choose. An alternative form of play is to give each student a copy of the game form. They write their individual answers on the form and total their points at the end. You can give prizes to those with the highest scores, or translate the scores into quiz grades.

11. Have individual students draw scenes from the book. Display the scenes and have the rest of the class look in their books to find the chapter or section that is being depicted. The first student to find the correct scene then displays his or her picture. When the game is over, collect the pictures and put them in a binder for students to look at during their free time.

NOTE: If students do not need the extra review, omit this lesson and go on to the test.

LESSON EIGHTEEN

Objective
To test the students' understanding of the main ideas and themes in *Night*

Activity #1
Distribute the *Night* Unit Tests. Go over the instructions in detail and allow the students the entire class period to complete the exam.

Activity #2
Collect all test papers and assigned books prior to the end of the class period.

QUIZ GAME *Night*

Section 1	Sections 2, 3	Section 4	Section 5	Sections 6, 7, 8, 9
100	100	100	100	100
200	200	200	200	200
300	300	300	300	300
400	400	400	400	400

This page is left blank for two-sided printing.

UNIT TESTS

NOTES ABOUT THE UNIT TESTS IN THIS UNIT:

There are 5 different unit tests which follow.

There are two short answer tests which are based primarily on facts from the novel. The answer key for short answer unit test 1 follows the student test. The answer key for short answer test 2 follows the student short answer unit test 2.

There is one advanced short answer unit test. It is based on the extra discussion questions. Use the matching key for short answer unit test 2 to check the matching section of the advanced short answer unit test. There is no key for the short answer questions. The answers will be based on the discussions you have had during class.

There are two multiple choice unit tests. Following the two unit tests, you will find an answer sheet on which students should mark their answers. The same answer sheet should be used for both tests; however, students' answers will be different for each test. Following the students' answer sheet for the multiple choice tests you will find your answer keys.

The short answer tests have a vocabulary section. You should choose 10 of the vocabulary words from this unit, read them orally and have the students write them down. Then, either have students write a definition or use the words in sentences. The second part of the vocabulary test is matching.

SHORT ANSWER UNIT TEST 1 *Night*

I. <u>Matching/ Identify</u>

_____ 1. Elie   A. survived to tell the story of the concentration camps
_____ 2. Chlomo   B. Rabbi who searched for his son
_____ 3. Martha   C. tormented Mr. Wiesel to get the gold crown
_____ 4. Juliek   D. offered the Wiesel family safe refuge
_____ 5. Franek   E. woman who had visions of the furnace fires
_____ 6. Meir Katz   F. trampled to death during the evacuation
_____ 7. Zalman   G. died at Buchenwald
_____ 8. Eliahou   H. Kapo who had bouts of madness
_____ 9. Idek   I. played Beethoven for the dying men
_____ 10. Schächter   J. died in the wagon

II. <u>Short Answer</u>

1. Summarize the story Moshe the Beadle told on his return from being deported. Why did he say he had returned to Sighet?

2. What did Elie do when the gypsy struck his father? Why? What was his father's response?

Short Answer Unit Test 1 *Night*

3. What did Elie Wiesel do when Idek hit his father? What was he thinking?

4. What was Elie's decision about fasting on Yom Kippur? Why did he make that decision?

5. Describe Elie's meeting with Juliek.

Short Answer Unit Test 1 *Night*

III. Fill-in-the-Blank

    Night is the autobiographical account of Elie Wiesel's time in the concentration camps in Europe during World War II. He grew up in the town of (1)_____, in the country of (2)_____. The people knew there was a war going on, but were not paying much attention. Even when (3)_____ returned to the town to tell his terrible tales of mass murders of Jews, the people would not believe it.. Elie tried to persuade his father to move to (4)_____ but his father would not do it. Even the news that the (5)_____ in Budapest were destroying Jewish shops and synagogues did not convince the people that danger was coming.

    During the Spring of 1944 the German army moved into the town. On the seventh day of (6)_____ the Germans arrested the leaders of the Jewish community. Soon after, two (7)_____ were set up and all of the Jewish people were made to move there. On the Saturday before (8)_____, Stern told the others they were to be deported.

    The train carrying the Wiesel family and their neighbors stopped first at (9)_____, which was the reception center for (10)_____. Elie was separated from his mother and sisters here, although he was able to stay with his father. They stayed in this camp for three weeks. Then they were forced to walk for four hours to another camp at (11)_____. Sometime around the end of January, 1945, the front drew near the camp. The prisoners were evacuated to (12)_____. They stayed at this camp for three days without food or water. Then they were taken by train to (13)_____. Chlomo Wiesel died here during the night of January 28, 1945. Elie stayed there in the children's block until the (14)_____ movement liberated the camp and the (15)_____ tanks arrived.

Short Answer Unit Test 1 *Night*

IV. <u>Essay</u>

Describe and analyze Elie Wiesel's changing view of God throughout the book.

Short Answer Unit Test 1 *Night*

V. Vocabulary Part 1

Listen to the vocabulary words and spell them. After you have spelled all the words, go back and write down the definitions.

WORD	**DEFINITION**
1._____	_____
2._____	_____
3._____	_____
4._____	_____
5._____	_____
6._____	_____
7._____	_____
8._____	_____
9._____	_____
10._____	_____

Vocabulary Part 2

Directions: Place the letter of the matching definition on the blank line.

_____ 1. anecdotes   A. necessary supplies, such as food
_____ 2. provisions   B. ashen; pallid
_____ 3. blandishments   C. boisterous and disorderly
_____ 4. sabotage   D. flattering comments
_____ 5. raucous   E. expressing sorrow
_____ 6. evacuation   F. withdrawing troops or civilians
_____ 7. bereaved   G. known widely and unfavorably; infamous
_____ 8. plaintive   H. left alone by death
_____ 9. livid   I. deliberate destruction
_____ 10. notorious   J. short accounts of humorous incidents

ANSWER KEY SHORT ANSWER UNIT TEST 1 *Night*

I. Matching/Identify
1. A
2. G
3. D
4. I
5. C
6. J
7. F
8. B
9. H
10. E

II. Short Answer
1. Summarize the story Moshe the Beadle told on his return from being deported. Why did he say he had returned to Sighet?

    He and the other foreign Jews had been taken by train through Hungary and into Poland. They were taken to a forest and made to dig graves. Then the Gestapo killed them. Moshe escaped because he had been mistaken for dead, although he was just wounded. He said he returned to tell the Jews to prepare themselves before it was too late.

2. What did Elie do when the gypsy struck his father? Why? What was his father's response? He did not do anything. He felt remorse, and thought he would never forgive the gypsy.
    His father whispered that the blow did not hurt.

3. What did Elie Wiesel do when Idek hit his father? What was he thinking?
    Elie did not do anything to help his father. He was trying to keep from getting hit himself. He was angry at his father for not avoiding Idek's punishment.

4. What was Elie's decision about fasting on Yom Kippur? Why did he make that decision? He did not fast. One reason was because he father had forbidden him to fast. The other reason was that he saw his gesture as an act of rebellion against God.

5. Describe Elie's meeting with Juliek.
    The prisoners had arrived at Gleiwitz, and were moving into the barracks. Men were pushing and trampling over each other. Elie heard a voice that he recognized. It was Juliek, the musician from Warsaw who had played the violin at Buna. They spoke for a few seconds. Juliek then played a Beethoven concerto on his violin. The next morning Juliek was dead and the violin had been trampled.

Answer Key Short Answer Unit Test 1 *Night*

III. Fill-in-the-Blank

Night is the autobiographical account of Elie Wiesel's time in the concentration camps in Europe during World War II. He grew up in the town of (1) **Sighet**, in the country of (2) **Transylvania**. The people knew there was a war going on, but were not paying much attention. Even when (3) **Moshe the Beadle** returned to the town to tell his terrible tales of mass murders of Jews, the people would not believe it.. Elie tried to persuade his father to move to (4) **Palestine**, but his father would not do it. Even the news that the (5) **Fascists** in Budapest were destroying Jewish shops and synagogues did not convince the people that danger was coming.

During the Spring of 1944 the German army moved into the town. On the seventh day of (6) **Passover** the Germans arrested the leaders of the Jewish community. Soon after, two (7) **ghettos** were set up and all of the Jewish people were made to move there. On the Saturday before (8) **Pentecost**, Stern told the others they were to be deported.

The train carrying the Wiesel family and their neighbors stopped first at (9) **Birkenau**, which was the reception center for (10) **Auschwitz**. Elie was separated from his mother and sisters here, although he was able to stay with his father. They stayed in this camp for three weeks. Then they were forced to walk for four hours to another camp at (11) **Buna**. Sometime around the end of January, 1945, the front drew near the camp. The prisoners were evacuated to (12) **Gleiwitz**. They stayed at this camp for three days without food or water. Then they were taken by train to (13) **Buchenwald**. Chlomo Wiesel died here during the night of January 28, 1945. Elie stayed there in the children's block until the (14) **resistance** movement liberated the camp and the (15) **American** tanks arrived.

IV. Essay

Describe and analyze Elie Wiesel's changing view of God throughout the book. Answers will vary depending on the class discussions.

V. Vocabulary Part 1

WORD	DEFINITION
1.	
2.	
3.	
4.	
5.	
6.	
7.	
8.	
9.	
10.	

Vocabulary Part 2

Directions: Place the letter of the matching definition on the blank line.

1. J
2. A
3. D
4. I
5. C
6. F
7. H
8. E
9. B
10. G

SHORT ANSWER UNIT TEST 2 *Night*

I. <u>Matching/ Identify</u>

_____ 1. selection   A. Elie did not do this for Yom Kippur.

_____ 2. bread   B. Each Jew had to wear a yellow one.

_____ 3. spoon   C. People threw some into the open train cars.

_____ 4. clean   D. Chlomo Wiesel died of this.

_____ 5. violin   E. The men did this before they evacuated.

_____ 6. star   F. Two were set up in Sighet.

_____ 7. ghettos   G. It was part of Elie's inheritance.

_____ 8. soup   H. It was crushed when Juliek died.

_____ 9. dysentery   I. Once it tasted like corpses.

_____ 10. fast   J. It was the gravest danger in the camps.

II. <u>Short Answer</u>

1. What was the setting and the year for the first section of the book? What was the world condition at the time?

2. Describe, in order, the events that happened from the last day of Passover until Pentecost.

Short Answer Unit Test 2 *Night*

3. To what did Wiesel compare the world?

4. When did Wiesel say the travelers left their illusions behind?

5. What were the only things in which Elie took an interest?

Short Answer Unit Test 2 *Night*

III. Fill-in-the-Blank

 Night is the autobiographical account of Elie Wiesel's time in the concentration camps in Europe during World War II. He grew up in the town of (1)_____, in the country of (2)_____. The people knew there was a war going on, but were not paying much attention. Even when (3)_____ returned to the town to tell his terrible tales of mass murders of Jews, the people would not believe it. Elie tried to persuade his father to move to (4)_____ but his father would not do it. Even the news that the (5)_____ in Budapest were destroying Jewish shops and synagogues did not convince the people that danger was coming.

 During the Spring of 1944 the German army moved into the town. On the seventh day of (6)_____ the Germans arrested the leaders of the Jewish community. Soon after, two (7)_____ were set up and all of the Jewish people were made to move there. On the Saturday before (8)_____, Stern told the others they were to be deported.

 The train carrying the Wiesel family and their neighbors stopped first at (9)_____, which was the reception center for (10)_____. Elie was separated from his mother and sisters here, although he was able to stay with his father. They stayed in this camp for three weeks. Then they were forced to walk for four hours to another camp at (11)_____. Sometime around the end of January, 1945, the front drew near the camp. The prisoners were evacuated to (12)_____. They stayed at this camp for three days without food or water. Then they were taken by train to (13)_____. Chlomo Wiesel died here during the night of January 28, 1945. Elie stayed there in the children's block until the (14)_____ movement liberated the camp and the (15)_____ tanks arrived.

Short Answer Unit Test 2 *Night*

IV. Essay

    The author often used vivid language to describe a scene or event. Give an example of his use of vivid language that you found most effective. Tell why it was effective.

Short Answer Unit Test 2 *Night*

V. Vocabulary

Listen to the vocabulary words and spell them. After you have spelled all the words, go back and write down the definitions.

WORD   **DEFINITION**

1. _____ _____
2. _____ _____
3. _____ _____
4. _____ _____
5. _____ _____
6. _____ _____
7. _____ _____
8. _____ _____
9. _____ _____
10. _____ _____

Vocabulary Part 2

Directions: Place the letter of the matching definition on the blank line.

_____ 1. treatise   A. grief; mourning
_____ 2. emigration   B. systematic, extensive written text
_____ 3. hermetically   C. the limit of one's resources or endurance
_____ 4. lucidity   D. clear understanding
_____ 5. frenzy   E. made thin due to starvation
_____ 6. torment   F. physical pain or mental anguish
_____ 7. lamentation   G. sealed against the entry or escape of air
_____ 8. emaciated   H. violent mental agitation or wild excitement
_____ 9. apathy   I. leaving one country for another
_____ 10. tether   J. lack of emotion or feeling

ANSWER KEY SHORT ANSWER UNIT TEST 2 *Night*

Note: Also use this key for the Advanced Short Answer Matching Test.
1. J
2. C
3. G
4. E
5. H
6. B
7. F
8. I
9. D
10. A

II. <u>Short Answer</u>
1. What was the setting and the year for the first section of the book? What was the world condition at the time?

    The year was 1942. The story started out in the town of Sighet in Transylvania. World War II was in progress. The author mentions 1943, then describes events in 1944. The Fascist party had taken power.

2. Describe, in order, the events that happened from the last day of Passover until Pentecost. On the seventh day of Passover the Germans arrested the Jewish community leaders. The Jewish residents were not allowed to leave their houses for three days. At the end of the three days the Jews had to start wearing the yellow star. Then two ghettos were set up. On the Saturday before Pentecost, Stern attended an extraordinary meeting of the council.
    When he returned he told the others they were all to be deported, starting the next day.

3. To what did Wiesel compare the world?

    He said it was a cattle wagon hermetically sealed.

4. When did Wiesel say the travelers left their illusions behind?

    It was when they left the train at Birkenau. They left their cherished objects and illusions behind on the train.

5. What were the only things in which Elie took an interest?

    He only took an interest in his soup and his crust of stale bread.

Answer Key Short Answer Unit Test 2 *Night*

III. Fill-in-the-Blank

Night is the autobiographical account of Elie Wiesel's time in the concentration camps in Europe during World War II. He grew up in the town of (1) **Sighet**, in the country of (2) **Transylvania**. The people knew there was a war going on, but were not paying much attention. Even when (3) **Moshe the Beadle** returned to the town to tell his terrible tales of mass murders of Jews, the people would not believe it.. Elie tried to persuade his father to move to (4) **Palestine**, but his father would not do it. Even the news that the (5) **Fascists** in Budapest were destroying Jewish shops and synagogues did not convince the people that danger was coming.

During the Spring of 1944 the German army moved into the town. On the seventh day of (6) **Passover** the Germans arrested the leaders of the Jewish community. Soon after, two (7) **ghettos** were set up and all of the Jewish people were made to move there. On the Saturday before (8) **Pentecost**, Stern told the others they were to be deported.

The train carrying the Wiesel family and their neighbors stopped first at (9) **Birkenau**, which was the reception center for (10) **Auschwitz**. Elie was separated from his mother and sisters here, although he was able to stay with his father. They stayed in this camp for three weeks. Then they were forced to walk for four hours to another camp at (11) **Buna**. Sometime around the end of January, 1945, the front drew near the camp. The prisoners were evacuated to (12) **Gleiwitz**. They stayed at this camp for three days without food or water. Then they were taken by train to (13) **Buchenwald**. Chlomo Wiesel died here during the night of January 28, 1945. Elie stayed there in the children's block until the (14) **resistance** movement liberated the camp and the (15) **American** tanks arrived.

IV. Essay

The author often used vivid language to describe a scene or event. Give an example of his use of vivid language that you found most effective. Tell why it was effective.

Answers will vary depending on the class discussions.

V. Vocabulary

	WORD	DEFINITION
1.	_____	_____
2.	_____	_____
3.	_____	_____
4.	_____	_____
5.	_____	_____
6.	_____	_____
7.	_____	_____
8.	_____	_____
9.	_____	_____
10.	_____	_____

Vocabulary Part 2

Directions: Place the letter of the matching definition on the blank line.
1. B
2. I
3. G
4. D
5. H
6. F
7. A
8. E
9. J

ADVANCED SHORT ANSWER UNIT TEST *Night*

I. <u>Matching/ Identify</u>

_____ 1. selection   A. Elie did not do this for Yom Kippur.

_____ 2. bread   B. Each Jew had to wear a yellow one.

_____ 3. spoon   C. People threw some into the open train cars.

_____ 4. clean   D. Chlomo Wiesel died of this.

_____ 5. violin   E. The men did this before they evacuated.

_____ 6. star   F. Two were set up in Sighet.

_____ 7. ghettos   G. It was part of Elie's inheritance.

_____ 8. soup   H. It was crushed when Juliek died.

_____ 9. dysentery   I. Once it tasted like corpses.

_____ 10. fast   J. It was the gravest danger in the camps.

II. <u>Short Answer</u>

1. In Section 4, Wiesel described the hanging of one young man. Then he said his soup was excellent that evening. What did he mean?

2. In Section 4, Wiesel described the hanging of the *pipel*, the young servant boy. He said the soup tasted of corpses that night. What did he mean?

Advanced Short Answer Unit Test *Night*

3. Describe and analyze Elie Wiesel's changing view of God throughout the book.

4. What was the overall mood of the story? Give examples to support your answer.

5. Is *Night* a good title for the book? Why or why not? If not, what title would you suggest?

Advanced Short Answer Unit Test *Night*

III. Quotations
Discuss the significance of the following quotations.

1. "Man raises himself toward God by the questions he asks Him," he was fond of repeating. "That is the true dialogue. Man questions God and God answers. But we don't understand His answers. We can't understand them. Because they come from the depths of the soul and they stay there until death. You will find the true answers, Eliezer, only within yourself!"

2. "The yellow star? Oh, well, what of it? You don't die of it . . . ."

3. "Men to the left! Women to the right!"

Advanced Short Answer Unit Test *Night*

4."Bite your lip, little brother. . . . don't cry. Keep your anger and your hatred for another day, for later on. The day will come, but not now. . . . Wait. Grit your teeth and wait."

5."Long live liberty! A curse upon Germany! A curse. . . . A cur--"

Advanced Short Answer Unit Test *Night*

IV. Vocabulary

Listen to the words and write them down. After you have written down all of the words, write a paragraph in which you use all of the words. The paragraph must in some way relates to *Night*.

1. _____
2. _____
3. _____
4. _____
5. _____

6. _____
7. _____
8. _____
9. _____
10. _____

MULTIPLE CHOICE UNIT TEST 1 *Night*

I. Matching/ Identify

_____ 1. Elie   A. survived to tell the story of the concentration camps

_____ 2. Chlomo   B. Rabbi who searched for his son

_____ 3. Martha   C. tormented Mr. Wiesel to get the gold crown

_____ 4. Juliek   D. offered the Wiesel family safe refuge

_____ 5. Franek   E. woman who had visions of the furnace fires

_____ 6. Meir Katz   F. trampled to death during the evacuation

_____ 7. Zalman   G. died at Buchenwald

_____ 8. Eliahou   H. Kapo who had bouts of madness

_____ 9. Idek   I. played Beethoven for the dying men

_____ 10. Schächter   J. died in the wagon

II. Multiple Choice

1. What did Moshe the Beadle tell the people on his return from being deported?
    A. The foreign Jews were made to dig coal to fill the large furnaces.
    B. The foreign Jews were shot and dumped into large mass graves.
    C. The foreign Jews were sent on a boat to Palestine.
    D. The foreign Jews who had money were able to buy their freedom.

2. What was the setting and the year for the first section of the book?
    A. 1935-1939 in Prague, Czechoslovakia
    B. 1950-1952 in Palestine and Jerusalem
    C. 1910-1915 in Berlin, Germany
    D. 1942-1944 in Sighet, Transylvania

3. To what did Wiesel compare the world?
    A. He compared it to a blind and deaf person.
    B. He compared it to a large hole in the ground.
    C. He compared it to a cattle wagon hermetically sealed.
    D. He compared it to the Bible story of the Jews in slavery in Egypt.

4. What did Madame Schächter see in her vision?
    A. She saw large open graves full of children.
    B. She saw a fire--a furnace, with huge flames.
    C. She saw row after row of empty houses.
    D. She saw the face of Hitler laughing at the entire world.

5. True or False: Elie beat up the gypsy who struck his father.
   A. True
   B. False

6. True or False: Elie gave up the gold crown to keep Franek from tormenting his father.
   A. True
   B. False

7. True or False: Elie said he observed the prayer service like a stranger.
   A. True
   B. False

8. What did Elie dream of when he dreamed of a better world?
   A. He imagined a world without German soldiers.
   B. He imagined a soup pot that was always full.
   C. He imagined all people living in peace.
   D. He imagined a world with no bells.

9. True or False: They were at Gleiwitz for three days. Then they traveled by train for ten days until they reached Buchenwald.
   A. True
   B. False

10. When did the first American troops arrive at the camp?
    A. 3 AM, May 5, 1946
    B. Midnight, June 1, 1945
    C. 6 PM, April 10, 1945
    D. 10 AM, March 30, 1947

Multiple Choice Unit Test 1 *Night*

III. Quotations

Directions: Match the quotation and its missing word or phrase.

_____ 1. "The yellow ___ ? Oh, well, what of it?"   A. Auschwitz

_____ 2. " ___ is not concerned with us."   B. listen

_____ 3. "Let the world hear of the existence of ___ ."   C. Jewish

_____ 4. "Look at it! A terrible ___ !"   D. God

_____ 5. "They're bombing ___!"   E. Buna

_____ 6. "Jews, ___ to me. It's all I ask of you."   F. star

_____ 7. "Yes, I am ___."   G. Hitler

_____ 8. "No! He isn't ___. Not yet!"   H. dead

_____ 9. "It's the end. ___ is no longer with us."   I. fire

_____ 10. "I've got more faith in ___ than in anyone else."   J. Humanity

IV. Vocabulary Part 1

_____ 1. anecdotes   A. people who are expelled from a country

_____ 2. deportees   B. sadness; depression

_____ 3. blandishments   C. boisterous and disorderly

_____ 4. sabotage   D. flattering comments

_____ 5. raucous   E. expressing sorrow

_____ 6. surname   F. a family name

_____ 7. bereaved   G. known widely and unfavorably; infamous

_____ 8. plaintive   H. left alone by death

_____ 9. melancholy   I. deliberate destruction

_____ 10. notorious   J. short accounts of humorous incidents

Multiple Choice Unit Test 1 *Night*

Vocabulary Part 2
Directions: Circle the letter next to the word that matches the definition.

11. **withdrawing troops or civilians**
    a. evacuation
    b. constraint
    c. emigration
    d. recesses

12. **necessary supplies, such as food**
    a. anecdotes
    b. dregs
    c. provisions
    d. notorious

13. **completely lacking or empty**
    a. deprive
    b. devoid
    c. bereaved
    d. elapsed

14. **clear understanding**
    a. apathy
    b. lucidity
    c. treatise
    d. blandishments

15. **to take something away from**
    a. deprive
    b. convoy
    c. monocle
    d. contagion

16. **returning to health after illness**
    a. bereaved
    b. convalescence
    c. melancholy
    d. feeble

17. **ashen; pallid**
    a. pestilential
    b. void
    c. insignificant
    d. livid

18. **second of two**
    a. surname
    b. recesses
    c. latter
    d. hermetically

19. **sadness; depression**
    a. frenzy
    b. constraint
    c. raucous
    d. melancholy

20. **the least desirable portions**
    a. elapsed
    b. recesses
    c. dregs
    d. apathy

MULTIPLE CHOICE UNIT TEST 2 *Night*

I. <u>Matching/ Identify</u>

_____ 1. selection   A. Elie did not do this for Yom Kippur.

_____ 2. bread   B. Each Jew had to wear a yellow one.

_____ 3. spoon   C. People threw some into the open train cars.

_____ 4. clean   D. Chlomo Wiesel died of this.

_____ 5. violin   E. The men did this before they evacuated.

_____ 6. star   F. Two were set up in Singhet.

_____ 7. ghettos   G. It was part of Elie's inheritance.

_____ 8. soup   H. It was crushed when Juliek died.

_____ 9. dysentery   I. Once it tasted like corpses.

_____ 10. fast   J. It was the gravest danger in the camps.

II. <u>Multiple Choice</u> 1. Which sentence does **not** describe Moshe the Beadle?

   A. He worked at the Hasidic synagogue.
   B. He was able to make himself seem insignificant, almost invisible.
   C. He was Aryan, not Jewish.
   D. He was timid, with dreamy eyes, and did not speak much.

2. What did Moshe the Beadle tell the people on his return from being deported?
   A. The foreign Jews were made to dig coal to fill the large furnaces.
   B. The foreign Jews were shot and dumped into large mass graves.
   C. The foreign Jews were sent on a boat to Palestine.
   D. The foreign Jews who had money were able to buy their freedom.

3. What was the setting and the year for the first section of the book?
   A. 1935-1939 in Prague, Czechoslovakia
   B. 1950-1952 in Palestine and Jerusalem
   C. 1910-1915 in Berlin, Germany
   D. 1942-1944 in Sighet, Transylvania

4. True or False: Elie's mother and sisters went to Martha's village.
   A. True
   B. False

Multiple Choice Unit Test 2 *Night*

5. Which statement is true?
    A. They went to Birkenau, then to Bergen-Belsen, the to Auschwitz.
    B. They stayed at Nuremberg for one month.
    C. They stayed at Galicia for six days, then went to Birkenau
    D. They were at Auschwitz for about three weeks. Then they went to Buna.

6. True or False: The dentist gave Elie a gold crown for one of his rotten teeth.
    A. True
    B. False

7. True or False: Elie said the men were more depressed than ever after the air raid.
    A. True
    B. False

8. When did the men hold their prayer service and wish each other a Happy New Year?
    A. on the eve of Rosh Hashana
    B. on the first day of Hanukkah
    C. on Yom Kippur
    D. on December 31

9. Why was his father giving Elie the inheritance?
    A. Mr. Wiesel had been selected. He was giving it to his son before his death.
    B. Mr. Wiesel thought Elie might be able to buy his freedom.
    C. Mr. Wiesel wanted Elie to be comfortable.
    D. Mr. Wiesel thought Elie had a better chance of hiding the things than he did.

10. What did Elie realize about Rabbi Eliahou's son just after the evacuation?
    A. The son was dead and the Rabbi could not admit it.
    B. The son had been trying to lose his father as the men were all running.
    C. The son had escaped and did not take his father.
    D. The son betrayed his father to get extra bread for himself.

Multiple Choice Unit Test 2 *Night*

III. Quotations
Directions: Match the quotation and its missing word or phrase.

_____ 1. "The yellow ___ ? Oh, well, what of it?"   A. Auschwitz

_____ 2. " _____ is not concerned with us."   B. concentration camp

_____ 3. "Let the world hear of the existence of ____ ."   C. Jewish

_____ 4. "Look at it! A terrible ___ !"   D. crematories

_____ 5. "They're bombing ___!"   E. Buna

_____ 6. "Don't forget you're in a ___."   F. star

_____ 7. "Yes, I am ___."   G. Hitler

_____ 8. Long live ___! A curse upon Germany!"   H. liberty

_____ 9. "Anything is possible. Even these ___ ."   I. fire

_____ 10. "I've got more faith in ___ than in anyone else."   J. humanity

IV. Vocabulary Part 1

_____ 1. treatise   A. grief; mourning

_____ 2. emigration   B. systematic, extensive written text

_____ 3. hermetically   C. the limit of one's resources or endurance

_____ 4. pestilential   D. likely to cause an epidemic disease

_____ 5. frenzy   E. made thin due to starvation

_____ 6. torment   F. physical pain or mental anguish

_____ 7. lamentation   G. sealed against the entry or escape of air

_____ 8. emaciated   H. violent mental agitation or wild excitement

_____ 9. apathy   I. leaving one country for another

_____ 10. tether   J. lack of emotion or feeling

Multiple Choice Unit Test 2 *Night*

Vocabulary Part 2
Directions: Circle the letter next to the word that matches the definition.

11. **clear understanding**
    a. apathy
    b. lucidity
    c. treatise
    d. blandishments

12. **to take something away from**
    a. deprive
    b. convoy
    c. monocle
    d. contagion

13. **beat; hit**
    a. sabotage
    b. livid
    c. constraint
    d. thrash

14. **a harmful influence**
    a. bereavement
    b. lamentation
    c. notorious
    d. contagion

15. **trivial; not important**
    a. monocle
    b. insignificant
    c. frenzy
    d. latter

16. **sadness; depression**
    a. frenzy
    b. constraint
    c. raucous
    d. melancholy

17. **the least desirable portions**
    a. elapsed
    b. recesses
    c. dregs
    d. apathy

18. **those expelled from a country**
    a. evacuated
    b. deportees
    c. monocle
    d. sabotage

19. **vigor; energy**
    a. lamentation
    b. raucous
    c. vitality
    d. profoundly

20. **left alone by death**
    a. bereaved
    b. contagion
    c. emaciated
    d. elapsed

ANSWER SHEET Multiple Choice Unit Tests
Night

I. Matching

1. _____
2. _____
3. _____
4. _____
5. _____
6. _____
7. _____
8. _____
9. _____
10. _____

II. Multiple Choice

1. (A) (B) (C) (D)
2. (A) (B) (C) (D)
3. (A) (B) (C) (D)
4. (A) (B) (C) (D)
5. (A) (B) (C) (D)
6. (A) (B) (C) (D)
7. (A) (B) (C) (D)
8. (A) (B) (C) (D)
9. (A) (B) (C) (D)
10. (A) (B) (C) (D)

III. Quotations

1. _____
2. _____
3. _____
4. _____
5. _____
6. _____
7. _____
8. _____
9. _____
10. _____

IV. Vocabulary

1. _____
2. _____
3. _____
4. _____
5. _____
6. _____
7. _____
8. _____
9. _____
10. _____
11. _____
12. _____
13. _____
14. _____
15. _____
16. _____
17. _____
18. _____
19. _____
20. _____

ANSWER SHEET KEY   Multiple Choice Unit Test 1
Night

I. Matching

1. A
2. G
3. D
4. I
5. C
6. J
7. F
8. B
9. H
10. E

II. Multiple Choice

1. (A) ( ) (C) (D)
2. (A) (B) (C) ( )
3. (A) (B) ( ) (D)
4. (A) ( ) (C) (D)
5. (A) ( ) (C) (D)
6. ( ) (B) (C) (D)
7. ( ) (B) (C) (D)
8. (A) (B) (C) ( )
9. ( ) (B) (C) (D)
10. (A) (B) ( ) (D)

III. Quotations

1. F
2. J
3. A
4. I
5. E
6. B
7. C
8. H
9. D
10. G

IV. Vocabulary

1. J
2. A
3. D
4. I
5. C
6. F
7. H
8. E
9. B
10. G
11. A
12. C
13. B
14. B
15. A
16. B
17. D
18. C
19. D
20. C

ANSWER SHEET   Multiple Choice Unit Test 2
Night

I. Matching

1. J
2. C
3. G
4. E
5. H
6. B
7. F
8. I
9. D
10. A

II. Multiple Choice

1. (A) (B) ( ) (D)
2. (A) ( ) (C) (D)
3. (A) (B) (C) ( )
4. (A) ( ) (C) (D)
5. (A) (B) (C) ( )
6. ( ) (B) (C) (D)
7. (A) ( ) (C) (D)
8. ( ) (B) (C) (D)
9. ( ) (B) (C) (D)
10. (A) ( ) (C) (D)

III. Quotations

1. F
2. J
3. A
4. I
5. E
6. B
7. C
8. H
9. D
10. G

IV. Vocabulary

1. B
2. I
3. G
4. D
5. H
6. F
7. A
8. E
9. J
10. C
11. B
12. A
13. D
14. D
15. B
16. D
17. C
18. B
19. C
20. A

UNIT RESOURCE MATERIALS

This page is left blank for two-sided printing.

BULLETIN BOARD IDEAS *Night*

1. Save one corner of the board for the best of students' writing assignments. You may want to use background maps of Europe to represent the setting of the novel.

2. Take one of the word search puzzles from the extra activities packet and with a marker copy it over in a large size on the bulletin board. Write the clue words to find to one side. Invite students prior to and after class to find the words and circle them on the bulletin board.

3. Have students find or draw pictures that they think resemble the people in the book.

4. Invite students to help make an interactive bulletin board quiz. Give each student a half-sheet of paper (about 4"x5") folded in half so that it can open. On the outside flap, have each student write a description of one of the characters in the text. On the inside, they will write the name of the character. You can staple or tack these papers to the bulletin board so that the students can read the descriptions and lift the flaps to find the answers.

5. Collect pictures of the area mentioned in the book.

6. Display articles about Elie Wiesel or the Holocaust.

7. Display a large map of Europe and have students mark the locations mentioned in the book.

EXTRA ACTIVITIES *Night*

One of the difficulties in teaching a novel is that all students don't read at the same speed. One student who likes to read may take the book home and finish it in a day or two. Sometimes a few students finish the in-class assignments early. The problem, then, is finding suitable extra activities for students.

Set up a library in the classroom. For this unit on *Night,* include other books by Elie Wiesel. There are also many other works dealing with World War II and the Holocaust that students could read. Several journals have critiques of Wiesel's works. Some of the students may enjoy reading these and responding either in writing or in discussion groups.

Your students who have reading difficulties, or speak English as a second language may benefit from listening to all or part of the book on tape.

Some students may like to draw. You might devise a contest or allow some extra-credit grade for students who draw characters or scenes from *Night.* Note, too, that if the students do not want to keep their drawings you may pick up some extra bulletin board materials this way. If you have a contest and you supply the prize. You could, possibly, make the drawing itself a non-refundable entry fee.

Have maps, a globe, and travel brochures on hand for easy reference. Travel agencies and automobile clubs are good sources for these materials.

The pages which follow contain games, puzzles, and worksheets. The keys, when appropriate, immediately follow the puzzle or worksheet. There are two main groups of activities: one group for the unit; that is, generally relating to the text, and another group of activities related strictly to the vocabulary. Directions for the games, puzzles, and worksheets are self-explanatory. The object here is to provide you with extra materials you may use in any way you choose.

MORE ACTIVITIES *Night*

1. Have students design a book cover (front and back and inside flaps) for *Night*.

2. Have students design a bulletin board (ready to be put up; not just sketched) for *Night*.

3. Use some of the related topics (noted earlier for an in-class library) as topics for research, reports, or written papers, or as topics for guest speakers.

4. Help students design and produce a talk show. Choose one of the story incidents as the topic. The host will interview the various characters. (Students should make up the questions they want the host to ask the characters.)

5. Have students work in pairs to create an interview with one of the characters. One student should be the interviewer and the other should be the interviewee. Students can work together to compose questions for the interviewer to ask. Each pair of students could present their interview to the class.

6. Invite students who have read other books by Elie Wiesel to present booktalks to the class.

7. Invite a member of a local synagogue to speak to the class about the Holocaust.

8. Have students hold small group discussions related to topics in the book. Assign a recorder and a speaker for each group. Have the speaker from each group make a report to the class.

9. Many areas now have museums dedicated to the Holocaust. If possible, visit one of these museums.

UNIT WORD SEARCH *Night*

```
U O Z F J P A U S C H W I T Z A E J A T F P N
Y G C C M L A Z C A P O C U E A O B P S C I B
O L T R B J A V B A I A Y R C J P I A T I G M
M E B R V L F W L H B N E Z X I A R S E O F S
K I R X M T A E J X A M A L G D T K S R Y I T
I W K A R G S N U Z U M W V S Q S E O N I O H
P I N F P T C E U R B F D L L B E N V V T S E
P T F N I Q I V D O Y O K F K Y G A E V I V N
U Z O N Z X S O W T Z I P O R A S U R D C A O
R M E K M Y T H X T D F Y M W T X N D J C U A
D S M Y T K S T P Q E S N O H P L A A I R F Y
T E H G N I S E G E A Q B L O Z K I R R B Z H
E L E G N E M E A H R U X H P W R E U R T P D
V G R A G M N B M I Y O L C S Y M O S E W Z U
U O Z F J P A U S C H W I T Z A E J A T F P N
```

SINGHET	DRUMER	PALESTINE	TRANSYLVANIA
ALPHONSE	PASSOVER	TZIPORA	CHLOMO
GESTAPO	FASCISTS	AMERICAN	YOMKIPPUR
BIRKENAU	KADDISH	ZALMAN	MENGELE
STERN	GLEIWITZ	BEETHOVEN	AUSCHWITZ

CROSSWORD *Night*

CROSSWORD CLUES *Night*

ACROSS
1. Elie did not do this on Yom Kippur
5. The prisoners ate this and soup
8. It once tasted like corpses
10. The reception center for Auschwitz
12. The only son
13. One Jew said he was the only one who had kept his promises
14. He tried to warn the Jews in Singhet: ___ the Beadle
17. The youngest of the Wiesel children
18. Elie had surgery on his ___
19. Dreamed of going to Haifa with Elie and Yossi
20. Mr. Wiesel didn't recognize this cousin
23. Akiba ___ thought God was testing the Jews
26. Elie's father's first name
28. They walked here from Auschwitz
29. A tradesman turned policeman
31. The men had to ___ the block before they evacuated
32. Jews had to wear the yellow ___
34. Elie's inheritance was a knife and a ___
35. The German security police
36. The country where Elie Wiesel grew up
37. The Kapo who had bouts of madness

DOWN
2. An ___ tank was at the gates of Buchenwald
3. The next eldest of the Wiesel children
4. A Polish boy who was trampled during the evacuation
6. The Jewish New Year: ___ Hashanah
7. This idea began to fascinate Elie during the evacuation
8. Woman who had a vision of the furnaces
9. Elie wanted his family to move here
10. Jewish musicians were not allowed to play this composer's music
11. This movement rescued the prisoners at Buchenwald
15. It ___ during the entire evacuation march
16. The Rabbi ___ was looking for his son
20. Elie Wiesel grew up in this town
21. German Jew who headed the block at Buna
22. The Germans arrested the Jewish leaders on the seventh day of ___
23. Mr. Wiesel had this ailment when he died
24. Elie saw this notorious doctor
25. They liberated the men in the hospital
27. Offered the family safe refuge in their village
28. Mr. Wiesel died in this camp
30. Elie and his father did not stay here, but joined the evacuation
33. Told Elie he had not been written down

CROSSWORD ANSWER KEY *Night*

MATCHING QUIZ/WORKSHEET 1 - Night

___ 1. HUNGARIAN   A. Elie wanted his family to move here

___ 2. SPOON   B. The Day of Atonement: Yom ___

___ 3. SNOWED   C. The country where Elie Wiesel grew up

___ 4. KIPPUR   D. Jewish musicians were not allowed to play this composer's music

___ 5. SCHACHTER   E. Elie had surgery on his ___

___ 6. BUNA   F. Had a sign that said 'Work is liberty!'

___ 7. VIOLIN   G. Elie's father's first name

___ 8. DYSENTERY   H. He tried to warn the Jews in Sighet: ___ the Beadle

___ 9. ELIE   I. It ___ during the entire evacuation march

___10. BEA   J. Elie's inheritance was a knife and a ___

___11. BEETHOVEN   K. The only son

___12. HILDA   L. Woman who had a vision of the furnaces

___13. AUSCHWITZ   M. Meir ___ died in the wagon

___14. CHLOMO   N. The next eldest of the Wiesel children

___15. HITLER   O. Elie hated these police first

___16. TRANSYLVANIA   P. It was crushed along with Juliek

___17. MOSHE   Q. Mr. Wiesel had this ailment when he died

___18. ZALMAN   R. Mr. Wiesel didn't recognize this cousin

___19. ELIAHOU   S. One Jew said he was the only one who had kept his promises

___20. PALESTINE   T. A Polish boy who was trampled during the evacuation

___21. FOOT   U. The eldest of the Wiesel children

___22. BIRKENAU   V. They walked here from Auschwitz

___23. DRUMER   W. The Rabbi ___ was looking for his son

___24. KATZ   X. Akiba ___ thought God was testing the Jews

___25. STEIN   Y. The reception center for Auschwitz

KEY: MATCHING QUIZ/WORKSHEET 1 - Night

O - 1. HUNGARIAN		A. Elie wanted his family to move here
J - 2. SPOON		B. The Day of Atonement: Yom ___
I - 3. SNOWED		C. The country where Elie Wiesel grew up
B - 4. KIPPUR		D. Jewish musicians were not allowed to play this composer's music
L - 5. SCHACHTER		E. Elie had surgery on his ___
V - 6. BUNA		F. Had a sign that said 'Work is liberty!'
P - 7. VIOLIN		G. Elie's father's first name
Q - 8. DYSENTERY		H. He tried to warn the Jews in Sighet: ___ the Beadle
K - 9. ELIE		I. It ___ during the entire evacuation march
N - 10. BEA		J. Elie's inheritance was a knife and a ___
D - 11. BEETHOVEN		K. The only son
U - 12. HILDA		L. Woman who had a vision of the furnaces
F - 13. AUSCHWITZ		M. Meir ___ died in the wagon
G - 14. CHLOMO		N. The next eldest of the Wiesel children
S - 15. HITLER		O. Elie hated these police first
C - 16. TRANSYLVANIA		P. It was crushed along with Juliek
H - 17. MOSHE		Q. Mr. Wiesel had this ailment when he died
T - 18. ZALMAN		R. Mr. Wiesel didn't recognize this cousin
W - 19. ELIAHOU		S. One Jew said he was the only one who had kept his promises
A - 20. PALESTINE		T. A Polish boy who was trampled during the evacuation
E - 21. FOOT		U. The eldest of the Wiesel children
Y - 22. BIRKENAU		V. They walked here from Auschwitz
X - 23. DRUMER		W. The Rabbi ___ was looking for his son
M - 24. KATZ		X. Akiba ___ thought God was testing the Jews
R - 25. STEIN		Y. The reception center for Auschwitz

MATCHING QUIZ/WORKSHEET 2 - Night

___ 1. HILDA A. Elie did not do this on Yom Kippur

___ 2. GHETTOS B. Akiba ___ thought God was testing the Jews

___ 3. SPOON C. It was the gravest danger

___ 4. SELECTION D. Dreamed of going to Haifa with Elie and Yossi

___ 5. ZALMAN E. Two ___ were set up in Sighet

___ 6. CLEAN F. They liberated the men in the hospital

___ 7. ALPHONSE G. Elie had surgery on his ___

___ 8. ROSH H. Played his violin for the dying men

___ 9. STERN I. The German security police

___ 10. SOUP J. He tormented Elie's father to get Elie's gold tooth

___ 11. FAST K. Told Elie he had not been written down

___ 12. FOOT L. The next eldest of the Wiesel children

___ 13. GESTAPO M. Elie hated these police first

___ 14. BEA N. Elie saw this notorious doctor

___ 15. YOSSI O. A Polish boy who was trampled during the evacuation

___ 16. RUSSIANS P. Elie's inheritance was a knife and a ___

___ 17. GLEIWITZ Q. The German Jew who headed the block at Buna

___ 18. TIBI R. It once tasted like corpses

___ 19. FRANEK S. The marchers' destination

___ 20. DYSENTERY T. Mr. Wiesel had this ailment when he died

___ 21. VIOLIN U. A tradesman turned policeman

___ 22. HUNGARIAN V. It was crushed along with Juliek

___ 23. DRUMER W. The men had to ___ the block before they evacuated

___ 24. JULIEK X. The eldest of the Wiesel children

___ 25. MENGELE Y. The Jewish New Year: ___ Hashanah

KEY: MATCHING QUIZ/WORKSHEET 2 - Night

X - 1. HILDA		A. Elie did not do this on Yom Kippur
E - 2. GHETTOS		B. Akiba ___ thought God was testing the Jews
P - 3. SPOON		C. It was the gravest danger
C - 4. SELECTION		D. Dreamed of going to Haifa with Elie and Yossi
O - 5. ZALMAN		E. Two ___ were set up in Sighet
W - 6. CLEAN		F. They liberated the men in the hospital
Q - 7. ALPHONSE		G. Elie had surgery on his ___
Y - 8. ROSH		H. Played his violin for the dying men
U - 9. STERN		I. The German security police
R - 10. SOUP		J. He tormented Elie's father to get Elie's gold tooth
A - 11. FAST		K. Told Elie he had not been written down
G - 12. FOOT		L. The next eldest of the Wiesel children
I - 13. GESTAPO		M. Elie hated these police first
L - 14. BEA		N. Elie saw this notorious doctor
K - 15. YOSSI		O. A Polish boy who was trampled during the evacuation
F - 16. RUSSIANS		P. Elie's inheritance was a knife and a ___
S - 17. GLEIWITZ		Q. The German Jew who headed the block at Buna
D - 18. TIBI		R. It once tasted like corpses
J - 19. FRANEK		S. The marchers' destination
T - 20. DYSENTERY		T. Mr. Wiesel had this ailment when he died
V - 21. VIOLIN		U. A tradesman turned policeman
M - 22. HUNGARIAN		V. It was crushed along with Juliek
B - 23. DRUMER		W. The men had to ___ the block before they evacuated
H - 24. JULIEK		X. The eldest of the Wiesel children
N - 25. MENGELE		Y. The Jewish New Year: ___ Hashanah

JUGGLE LETTER REVIEW GAME CLUE SHEET 1 - *Night*

1. WENODS = 1. _____
It __ during the entire evacuation march

2. OSNOP = 2. _____
Elie's inheritance was a knife and a ___

3. SSNUIRAS = 3. _____
They liberated the men in the hospital

4. OHSR = 4. _____
The Jewish New Year: ___ Hashanah

5. EELI = 5. _____
The only son

6. SRAPVOSE = 6. _____
The Germans arrested the Jewish leaders on the seventh day of ___

7. RFNAEK = 7. _____
He tormented Elie's father to get Elie's gold tooth

8. ELIRHT = 8. _____
One Jew said he was the only one who had kept his promises

9. EMURRD = 9. _____
Akiba ___ thought God was testing the Jews

10. POSU =10. _____
It once tasted like corpses

11. LAZNMA =11. _____
A Polish boy who was trampled during the evacuation

12. WCTUHAISZ =12. _____
Had a sign that said 'Work is liberty!'

13. FOTO =13. _____
Elie had surgery on his ___

14. AARHTM =14. _____
Offered the family safe refuge in her village

15. RBADE =15. _____
The prisoners ate this and soup

16. UPIPRK =16._____
The Day of Atonement: Yom ___

17. RSCHHACET =17._____
Woman who had a vision of the furnaces

18. ELJUKI =18._____
Played his violin for the dying men

19. RSTA =19._____
Jews had to wear the yellow ___

20. RPAZITO =20._____
The youngest of the Wiesel children

21. ELOPNSHA =21._____
The German Jew who headed the block at Buna

22. TENASLEIP =22._____
Elie wanted his family to move here

23. TENSR =23._____
A tradesman turned policeman

24. ATGPOES =24._____
The German security police

25. AUIELHO =25._____
The Rabbi ___ was looking for his son

26. TRNYEDEYS =26._____
Mr. Wiesel had this ailment when he died

27. OEHSM =27._____
He tried to warn the Jews in Sighet: ___ the Beadle

28. LCHOOM =28._____
Elie's father's first name

KEY: JUGGLE LETTER REVIEW GAME CLUE SHEET 1 - *Night*

1. WENODS = 1. SNOWED
   It ___ during the entire evacuation march

2. OSNOP = 2. SPOON
   Elie's inheritance was a knife and a ___

3. SSNUIRAS = 3. RUSSIANS
   They liberated the men in the hospital

4. OHSR = 4. ROSH
   The Jewish New Year: ___ Hashanah

5. EELI = 5. ELIE
   The only son

6. SRAPVOSE = 6. PASSOVER
   The Germans arrested the Jewish leaders on the seventh day of ___

7. RFNAEK = 7. FRANEK
   He tormented Elie's father to get Elie's gold tooth

8. ELIRHT = 8. HITLER
   One Jew said he was the only one who had kept his promises

9. EMURRD = 9. DRUMER
   Akiba ___ thought God was testing the Jews

10. POSU = 10. SOUP
    It once tasted like corpses

11. LAZNMA = 11. ZALMAN
    A Polish boy who was trampled during the evacuation

12. WCTUHAISZ = 12. AUSCHWITZ
    Had a sign that said 'Work is liberty!'

13. FOTO = 13. FOOT
    Elie had surgery on his ___

14. AARHTM = 14. MARTHA
    Offered the family safe refuge in her village

15. RBADE = 15. BREAD
    The prisoners ate this and soup

16. UPIPRK =16. KIPPUR
The Day of Atonement: Yom ___

17. RSCHHACET =17. SCHACHTER
Woman who had a vision of the furnaces

18. ELJUKI =18. JULIEK
Played his violin for the dying men

19. RSTA =19. STAR
Jews had to wear the yellow ___

20. RPAZITO =20. TZIPORA
The youngest of the Wiesel children

21. ELOPNSHA =21. ALPHONSE
The German Jew who headed the block at Buna

22. TENASLEIP =22. PALESTINE
Elie wanted his family to move here

23. TENSR =23. STERN
A tradesman turned policeman

24. ATGPOES =24. GESTAPO
The German security police

25. AUIELHO =25. ELIAHOU
The Rabbi ___ was looking for his son

26. TRNYEDEYS =26. DYSENTERY
Mr. Wiesel had this ailment when he died

27. OEHSM =27. MOSHE
He tried to warn the Jews in Sighet: ___ the Beadle

28. LCHOOM =28. CHLOMO
Elie's father's first name

JUGGLE LETTER REVIEW GAME CLUE SHEET 2 - *Night*

1. SFTA = 1. _____
   Elie did not do this on Yom Kippur

2. ELGMEEN = 2. _____
   Elie saw this notorious doctor

3. MAIANRCE = 3. _____
   An ___ tank was at the gates of Buchenwald

4. AENCIRESST = 4. _____
   This movement rescued the prisoners at Buchenwald

5. AEB = 5. _____
   The next eldest of the Wiesel children

6. SFSCTAIS = 6. _____
   They attacked Jewish shops and synagogues

7. UIRAAHGNN = 7. _____
   Elie hated these police first

8. NSEIT = 8. _____
   Mr. Wiesel didn't recognize this cousin

9. OCTNEISLE = 9. _____
   It was the gravest danger

10. IGNYD =10. _____
    This idea began to fascinate Elie during the evacuation

11. IELTGWZI =11. _____
    The marchers' destination

12. NECLA =12. _____
    The men had to ___ the block before they evacuated

13. THSGOTE =13. _____
    Two ___ were set up in Sighet

14. SSIOY =14. _____
    Told Elie he had not been written down

15. HIDAKSD =15. _____
    The men recited this prayer for themselves

16. ALHDI =16._____
The eldest of the Wiesel children

17. IBTI =17._____
Dreamed of going to Haifa with Elie and Yossi

18. KARBUNEI =18._____
The reception center for Auschwitz

19. ENUWALBHCD =19._____
Mr. Wiesel died in this camp

20. AOTIHSLP =20._____
Elie and his father did not stay here, but joined the evacuation

21. ILINOV =21._____
It was crushed along with Juliek

22. ALVRSTINAYNA =22._____
The country where Elie Wiesel grew up

23. TSHEGI =23._____
Elie Wiesel grew up in this town

24. AKTZ =24._____
Meir ___ died in the wagon

25. EKID =25._____
The Kapo who had bouts of madness

26. NUAB =26._____
They walked here from Auschwitz

KEY: JUGGLE LETTER REVIEW GAME CLUE SHEET 2 - *Night*

1. SFTA = 1. FAST
   Elie did not do this on Yom Kippur

2. ELGMEEN = 2. MENGELE
   Elie saw this notorious doctor

3. MAIANRCE = 3. AMERICAN
   An ___ tank was at the gates of Buchenwald

4. AENCIRESST = 4. RESISTANCE
   This movement rescued the prisoners at Buchenwald

5. AEB = 5. BEA
   The next eldest of the Wiesel children

6. SFSCTAIS = 6. FASCISTS
   They attacked Jewish shops and synagogues

7. UIRAAHGNN = 7. HUNGARIAN
   Elie hated these police first

8. NSEIT = 8. STEIN
   Mr. Wiesel didn't recognize this cousin

9. OCTNEISLE = 9. SELECTION
   It was the gravest danger

10. IGNYD = 10. DYING
    This idea began to fascinate Elie during the evacuation

11. IELTGWZI = 11. GLEIWITZ
    The marchers' destination

12. NECLA = 12. CLEAN
    The men had to ___ the block before they evacuated

13. THSGOTE = 13. GHETTOS
    Two ___ were set up in Sighet

14. SSIOY = 14. YOSSI
    Told Elie he had not been written down

15. HIDAKSD = 15. KADDISH
    The men recited this prayer for themselves

16. ALHDI =16. HILDA
The eldest of the Wiesel children

17. IBTI =17. TIBI
Dreamed of going to Haifa with Elie and Yossi

18. KARBUNEI =18. BIRKENAU
The reception center for Auschwitz

19. ENUWALBHCD =19. BUCHENWALD
Mr. Wiesel died in this camp

20. AOTIHSLP =20. HOSPITAL
Elie and his father did not stay here, but joined the evacuation

21. ILINOV =21. VIOLIN
It was crushed along with Juliek

22. ALVRSTINAYNA =22. TRANSYLVANIA
The country where Elie Wiesel grew up

23. TSHEGI =23. SIGHET
Elie Wiesel grew up in this town

24. AKTZ =24. KATZ
Meir ___ died in the wagon

25. EKID =25. IDEK
The Kapo who had bouts of madness

26. NUAB =26. BUNA
They walked here from Auschwitz

VOCABULARY RESOURCE MATERIALS

VOCABULARY WORD SEARCH *Night*

All the words in this puzzle are associated with *Night* with emphasis on the vocabulary words being studied in the unit. The words are placed backwards, forward, diagonally, up and down. The words used in the puzzle are listed below.

```
R E C A C O E Y A B X D F E K Y M R Y X J G J J Z G D K Z Y
N M Z N O A N T Y O L E P W W P L T H O N I C S A F P X Z O
D A O E N V C I W L A A C M R R P L T O V J Q M O J E N Z D
U N D C S X U D X M D O N U D O P H A L E N P E N Z E T M K
T U G O R Z B C B V H N U Y I I E A D R I X T C F R G O Z K
D S F T A M E U A A A N D O B S F E D T M T C W V J N H P B
E I J E I G R L Y C Q R I W F I H O H E K L E T O F K X Z Y
C M G S N B E T I W E R O J V O J M L A D Y K M Y M D M B H
S U I U T S D F O S L Y V X D N R A E I G P W S R A P Q G K
C T U G C R I P U R O Z E M Y S N P V N U Y E J N E T K J X
M C R E R N G O I V M F D I G C Q I E P T E Q H B F H G H I
E M N E G A I B E C F E H W H B W U L V T S D G K B C M T O
B T C I A R T H E L C O N O M X T H W R B C P H I L P A Z Q
J Z S K O T Q I D X Y W L T J J C K O U O N A S A A R B H J
B N H T S K I N O E U Y E M G Z A P U A O M X W D Y G P H M
I I O P L M V S B N R Z L Q T S E F Z K M K F M A R O T O A
V N X I Y Z L D E J H A F P H D S M W H M I I P C U Q I K A
O C H U S U N V L A I T N E L I T S E P Z S B E N P G A I B
```

SURNAME	MELANCHOLY	MONOCLE
ENCUMBERED	CONSTRAINT	LUCIDITY
INSIGNIFICANT	PROVISIONS	CONVALESCENT
PROFOUNDLY	HERMETICALLY	BLANDISHMENTS
DEPORTEES	PESTILENTIAL	CONVOY
EMIGRATION	NOTORIOUS	FRENZY
TREATISE	DEVOID	TORMENT
ANECDOTES		

VOCABULARY CROSSWORD *Night*

VOCABULARY CROSSWORD CLUES *Night*

ACROSS
1 Those being expelled from a country
2 Passed
5 Restriction
8 Left alone by death
11 Short, humorous stories
14 Emptiness
15 Ashen; pallid
17 An eyeglass for one eye
19 Lacking strength
20 Vigor; energy
22 Made thin due to starvation
23 To cause physical pain or mental anguish
24 Sadness; depression
25 Beat; hit

DOWN
1 To take something away from
3 Second of two
4 Remote, secret places
5 A harmful influence
6 Trivial; not important
7 The limit of one's resources or endurance
8 Coaxing by flattery
9 Lack of emotion or feeling
10 Returning to health after an illness
12 Completely lacking or empty
13 Treacherous action to defeat a cause
15 Grief; mourning
16 A group of vehicles traveling together
18 Clear understanding
19 Violent mental agitation or wild excitement
21 The least desirable portions

VOCABULARY CROSSWORD ANSWER KEY *Night*

Across / Down entries filled in grid:

- DEPORTEES
- ELAPSED
- CONSTRAINT
- BEREAVED
- ANECDOTES
- VOID
- LIVID
- FEEBLE
- VITALITY
- EMACIATED
- TORMENT
- MELANCHOLY
- THRASH

Down words visible:
- DEPLORABLE
- CONVALESCENTS
- CAVED IN
- REPRIEVE
- ANTECHAMBER
- CONDOLENCES
- CATASTROPHY
- ANECDOTES
- AGITATION
- SABOTAGE
- LAMENT
- VITALITY
- PACIFIC
- ETHEREAL
- INSIGNIA
- ATESTER
- LUCIDITY
- FRENZY
- VOYAGE

VOCABULARY WORKSHEET 1 - Night

___ 1. NOTORIOUS   A. Known unfavorably

___ 2. ENCUMBERED   B. Emptiness

___ 3. MONOCLE   C. The limit of one's resources or endurance

___ 4. FEEBLE   D. Restriction

___ 5. CONVALESCENT   E. Trivial; not important

___ 6. CONSTRAINT   F. Vigor; energy

___ 7. APATHY   G. A group of vehicles traveling together

___ 8. CONTAGION   H. Returning to health after an illness

___ 9. RAUCOUS   I. A harmful influence

___10. TETHER   J. Boisterous and disorderly

___11. DEPORTEES   K. Withdrawing troops or civilians from an area

___12. LUCIDITY   L. Clear understanding

___13. SABOTAGE   M. Written discussion of a topic

___14. INSIGNIFICANT   N. Absolutely; in an unqualified way

___15. EVACUATION   O. Made thin due to starvation

___16. PROFOUNDLY   P. Coaxing by flattery

___17. VOID   Q. Short, humorous stories

___18. CONVOY   R. Treacherous action to defeat a cause

___19. BLANDISHMENTS   S. Lacking strength

___20. TREATISE   T. An eyeglass for one eye

___21. RELENTLESSLY   U. Steadily; persistently

___22. EMACIATED   V. To cause physical pain or mental anguish

___23. ANECDOTES   W. Lack of emotion or feeling

___24. VITALITY   X. Those being expelled from a country

___25. TORMENT   Y. Hindered; restricted

KEY: VOCABULARY WORKSHEET 1 - *Night*

A - 1. NOTORIOUS		A. Known unfavorably
Y - 2. ENCUMBERED		B. Emptiness
T - 3. MONOCLE		C. The limit of one's resources or endurance
S - 4. FEEBLE		D. Restriction
H - 5. CONVALESCENT		E. Trivial; not important
D - 6. CONSTRAINT		F. Vigor; energy
W - 7. APATHY		G. A group of vehicles traveling together
I - 8. CONTAGION		H. Returning to health after an illness
J - 9. RAUCOUS		I. A harmful influence
C - 10. TETHER		J. Boisterous and disorderly
X - 11. DEPORTEES		K. Withdrawing troops or civilians from an area
L - 12. LUCIDITY		L. Clear understanding
R - 13. SABOTAGE		M. Written discussion of a topic
E - 14. INSIGNIFICANT		N. Absolutely; in an unqualified way
K - 15. EVACUATION		O. Made thin due to starvation
N - 16. PROFOUNDLY		P. Coaxing by flattery
B - 17. VOID		Q. Short, humorous stories
G - 18. CONVOY		R. Treacherous action to defeat a cause
P - 19. BLANDISHMENTS		S. Lacking strength
M - 20. TREATISE		T. An eyeglass for one eye
U - 21. RELENTLESSLY		U. Steadily; persistently
O - 22. EMACIATED		V. To cause physical pain or mental anguish
Q - 23. ANECDOTES		W. Lack of emotion or feeling
F - 24. VITALITY		X. Those being expelled from a country
V - 25. TORMENT		Y. Hindered; restricted

VOCABULARY WORKSHEET 2 - *Night*

___ 1. PESTILENTIAL A. Likely to cause an epidemic disease

___ 2. FEEBLE B. An eyeglass for one eye

___ 3. BEREAVED C. Boisterous and disorderly

___ 4. EMACIATED D. Beat; hit

___ 5. DEVOID E. Family name

___ 6. TORMENT F. Ashen; pallid

___ 7. LAMENTATION G. The limit of one's resources or endurance

___ 8. RAUCOUS H. Grief; mourning

___ 9. TETHER I. A harmful influence

___ 10. TREATISE J. Absolutely; in an unqualified way

___ 11. FRENZY K. Made thin due to starvation

___ 12. SABOTAGE L. Withdrawing troops or civilians from an area

___ 13. INSIGNIFICANT M. Treacherous action to defeat a cause

___ 14. THRASH N. Sealed against the entry or escape of air

___ 15. EVACUATION O. Written discussion of a topic

___ 16. DEPORTEES P. To cause physical pain or mental anguish

___ 17. MONOCLE Q. Known unfavorably

___ 18. DEPRIVE R. Left alone by death

___ 19. PROFOUNDLY S. Those being expelled from a country

___ 20. DREGS T. To take something away from

___ 21. CONTAGION U. Lacking strength

___ 22. HERMETICALLY V. Violent mental agitation or wild excitement

___ 23. LIVID W. Completely lacking or empty

___ 24. SURNAME X. The least desirable portions

___ 25. NOTORIOUS Y. Trivial; not important

KEY: VOCABULARY WORKSHEET 2 - *Night*

A - 1. PESTILENTIAL		A. Likely to cause an epidemic disease
U - 2. FEEBLE		B. An eyeglass for one eye
R - 3. BEREAVED		C. Boisterous and disorderly
K - 4. EMACIATED		D. Beat; hit
W - 5. DEVOID		E. Family name
P - 6. TORMENT		F. Ashen; pallid
H - 7. LAMENTATION		G. The limit of one's resources or endurance
C - 8. RAUCOUS		H. Grief; mourning
G - 9. TETHER		I. A harmful influence
O - 10. TREATISE		J. Absolutely; in an unqualified way
V - 11. FRENZY		K. Made thin due to starvation
M - 12. SABOTAGE		L. Withdrawing troops or civilians from an area
Y - 13. INSIGNIFICANT		M. Treacherous action to defeat a cause
D - 14. THRASH		N. Sealed against the entry or escape of air
L - 15. EVACUATION		O. Written discussion of a topic
S - 16. DEPORTEES		P. To cause physical pain or mental anguish
B - 17. MONOCLE		Q. Known unfavorably
T - 18. DEPRIVE		R. Left alone by death
J - 19. PROFOUNDLY		S. Those being expelled from a country
X - 20. DREGS		T. To take something away from
I - 21. CONTAGION		U. Lacking strength
N - 22. HERMETICALLY		V. Violent mental agitation or wild excitement
F - 23. LIVID		W. Completely lacking or empty
E - 24. SURNAME		X. The least desirable portions
Q - 25. NOTORIOUS		Y. Trivial; not important

VOCABULARY JUGGLE LETTER REVIEW GAME CLUE SHEET - Night

1. LAELCHMERTIY = 1. _____
   Sealed against the entry or escape of air

2. PDRIVEE = 2. _____
   To take something away from

3. HSNNEISLBDTAM = 3. _____
   Coaxing by flattery

4. ETHERT = 4. _____
   The limit of one's resources or endurance

5. NROOUYDFPL = 5. _____
   Absolutely; in an unqualified way

6. CTGIANOON = 6. _____
   A harmful influence

7. RTSIAETE = 7. _____
   Written discussion of a topic

8. AYVTTIIL = 8. _____
   Vigor; energy

9. HARHST = 9. _____
   Beat; hit

10. DEODVI =10. _____
    Completely lacking or empty

11. NTLAAEMITON =11. _____
    Grief; mourning

12. SOOOUTRIN =12. _____
    Known unfavorably

13. PROEEETSD =13. _____
    Those being expelled from a country

14. SPLIEENIATTL =14. _____
    Likely to cause an epidemic disease

15. UEAITANVCO =15. _____
    Withdrawing troops or civilians from an area

16. TORCATSNIN =16. _____
    Restriction

17. EPEALSD =17. _____
Passed

18. ACEAETIDM =18. _____
Made thin due to starvation

19. RNMAESU =19. _____
Family name

20. TELATR =20. _____
Second of two

21. NCOOVY =21. _____
A group of vehicles traveling together

22. UOCSRAU =22. _____
Boisterous and disorderly

23. IDIVL =23. _____
Ashen; pallid

24. VSCLNNAECTEO =24. _____
Returning to health after an illness

25. AEOTAGBS =25. _____
Treacherous action to defeat a cause

26. UEBEDMRENC =26. _____
Hindered; restricted

27. TPYAAH =27. _____
Lack of emotion or feeling

28. IOVD =28. _____
Emptiness

29. SSRSCEEE =29. _____
Remote, secret places

30. ENMLOOC =30. _____
An eyeglass for one eye

31. TLRLESSNEYEL =31. _____
Steadily; persistently

32. CTYULIDI =32. _____
Clear understanding

33. TODSNEECA =33. _____
Short, humorous stories

34. NTETRMO =34. _____
To cause physical pain or mental anguish

35. DVBEEREA =35. _____
Left alone by death

36. NFINTCAIINGSI =36. _____
Trivial; not important

37. CAOEHYLMNL =37. _____
Sadness; depression

38. YNFERZ =38. _____
Violent mental agitation or wild excitement

39. SRGDE =39. _____
The least desirable portions

40. EFEELB =40. _____
Lacking strength

41. ROVPSIONIS =41. _____
Necessary supplies, such as food

KEY: VOCABULARY JUGGLE LETTER REVIEW GAME CLUE SHEET - *Night*

1. LAELCHMERTIY = 1. HERMETICALLY
   Sealed against the entry or escape of air

2. PDRIVEE = 2. DEPRIVE
   To take something away from

3. HSNNEISLBDTAM = 3. BLANDISHMENTS
   Coaxing by flattery

4. ETHERT = 4. TETHER
   The limit of one's resources or endurance

5. NROOUYDFPL = 5. PROFOUNDLY
   Absolutely; in an unqualified way

6. CTGIANOON = 6. CONTAGION
   A harmful influence

7. RTSIAETE = 7. TREATISE
   Written discussion of a topic

8. AYVTTIIL = 8. VITALITY
   Vigor; energy

9. HARHST = 9. THRASH
   Beat; hit

10. DEODVI = 10. DEVOID
    Completely lacking or empty

11. NTLAAEMITON = 11. LAMENTATION
    Grief; mourning

12. SOOOUTRIN = 12. NOTORIOUS
    Known unfavorably

13. PROEEETSD = 13. DEPORTEES
    Those being expelled from a country

14. SPLIEENIATTL = 14. PESTILENTIAL
    Likely to cause an epidemic disease

15. UEAITANVCO = 15. EVACUATION
    Withdrawing troops or civilians from an area

16. TORCATSNIN = 16. CONSTRAINT
    Restriction

17. EPEALSD =17. ELAPSED
Passed

18. ACEAETIDM =18. EMACIATED
Made thin due to starvation

19. RNMAESU =19. SURNAME
Family name

20. TELATR =20. LATTER
Second of two

21. NCOOVY =21. CONVOY
A group of vehicles traveling together

22. UOCSRAU =22. RAUCOUS
Boisterous and disorderly

23. IDIVL =23. LIVID
Ashen; pallid

24. VSCLNNAECTEO =24. CONVALESCENT
Returning to health after an illness

25. AEOTAGBS =25. SABOTAGE
Treacherous action to defeat a cause

26. UEBEDMRENC =26. ENCUMBERED
Hindered; restricted

27. TPYAAH =27. APATHY
Lack of emotion or feeling

28. IOVD =28. VOID
Emptiness

29. SSRSCEEE =29. RECESSES
Remote, secret places

30. ENMLOOC =30. MONOCLE
An eyeglass for one eye

31. TLRLESSNEYEL =31. RELENTLESSLY
Steadily; persistently

32. CTYULIDI =32. LUCIDITY
Clear understanding

33. TODSNEECA =33. ANECDOTES
Short, humorous stories

34. NTETRMO =34. TORMENT
To cause physical pain or mental anguish

35. DVBEEREA =35. BEREAVED
Left alone by death

36. NFINTCAIINGSI =36. INSIGNIFICANT
Trivial; not important

37. CAOEHYLMNL =37. MELANCHOLY
Sadness; depression

38. YNFERZ =38. FRENZY
Violent mental agitation or wild excitement

39. SRGDE =39. DREGS
The least desirable portions

40. EFEELB =40. FEEBLE
Lacking strength

41. ROVPSIONIS =41. PROVISIONS
Necessary supplies, such as food